DATE DUE

Waiting for the Wind

TRANSLATIONS FROM THE ASIAN CLASSICS

権中納言定家

み乃瀬人の
かむ乃瀬の名りのゆき
てやるもかし
ほの身もこ
う羇集ぃこ

Waiting for the Wind

THIRTY-SIX POETS OF JAPAN'S
LATE MEDIEVAL AGE

TRANSLATED AND WITH AN INTRODUCTION BY
Steven D. Carter

COLUMBIA UNIVERSITY PRESS   NEW YORK

COLUMBIA UNIVERSITY PRESS
NEW YORK   CHICHESTER, WEST SUSSEX

Includes index.
ISBN 0-231-06854-9
ISBN 0-231-06855-7 (pbk.)
1. Waka—Translations into English.
2. Waka, English—Translations from Japanese.
3. Japanese poetry—1185–1500—Translations into English.
4. English poetry—Translations from Japanese.
I. Carter, Steven D.   II. Series.
PL782.E3W25 1989
895.6′12′08—dc19   89-30578
                          CIP

Printed in the United States of America

Book design by Charles B. Hames

Casebound editions of Columbia University Press books are
printed on permanent and durable acid-free paper.

to HCM

Translations from the Asian Classics

CONTENTS

vii

PREFACE

In recent years, Western readers of the Japanese *uta*—the thirty-one-syllable lyric that was the major genre of court poetry throughout its history—have been introduced to most of the major poets of that form in English translation, from the early bards of the Yamato and Nara (710–784) eras to the courtier and priest poets of the Heian (794–1185) and early Kamakura periods (1185–1250). Amid this flurry of activity, however, one very important era of the classical uta tradition has been almost totally neglected—the late medieval period, comprising the years 1250–1500. This book is intended as a beginning step toward bridging that gap.

By 1250, the uta form was already over half a millennium old, and scholars have suggested that it was becoming a tired genre, weighed down with conventions that made originality difficult. Yet the fact remains that the uta continued to be the main form of Japanese poetry for another two-hundred and fifty years, during which time a number of fine poets still found it possible to express themselves within the vocabulary of an ancient tradition. Some departed from the standards of the past only rarely, while others did so more often and with greater vigor, as the introduction to the translations will, I hope, make clear. All enriched the poetic heritage in ways that influenced later poets writing in newer genres now fairly familiar to Western readers—including Sōgi (1421–1502) and other poets of linked verse (*renga*), and the *haikai* poets Bashō (1644–1694) and Buson (1716–1783).

The uta of the late medieval age share much with the poetry

of the *Shin kokinshū* (New Collection of Ancient and Modern Times, 1206), eighth of the imperial collections of the genre, and the one to which many poets of later years looked for their inspiration. The concept of *sabi*, or quiet solitude, for instance, was as crucial to the poetic stance of many poets writing in the mid-fourteenth century as it had been to Saigyō (1118–1190); and *ushin*, the aesthetic of intense feeling so important to Fujiwara no Teika (1162–1241) in his last years, was a guiding principle for later poets too. Indeed, the late medieval period was profoundly nostalgic in its sensibility, looking always to the past for its standards, particularly to Teika himself. The variety of poetic attitudes and approaches they found within his opus did much to define the structure of late medieval theory and praxis.

The poems of the late Kamakura and Muromachi ages also have positive virtues, some of which are seldom found in earlier periods: the imagistic realism of the Kyōgoku-Reizei poets, for example, or the great tonal resonance of the informal poems of a monk-poet like Yoshida no Kenkō (b. 1283). Ultimately, it is for these qualities that the poems of the late medieval age deserve the attention of anyone interested in the special beauties of the uta form and of lovers of poetry in general.

For her many suggestions toward improvement of the translations appearing in this book I owe a special debt to my wife Mary, as I do to Edward Peng for helping prepare and edit the manuscript. Also due thanks are my editors at Columbia University Press, Jennifer Crewe and Ann Miller, whose labors have improved the manuscript greatly. Finally, a word of gratitude goes to the College of Humanities, Brigham Young University, for a sum of money offered to assist toward publication.

INTRODUCTION

In his delightful book *The Fine Art of Literary Mayhem*, Myrick Land recounts the history of that most rarefied form of warfare, the literary dispute, beginning with battles involving the ever-irascible Samuel Johnson and his unhappy opponents, and ending with less colorful but equally intense feuds between more modern combatants—F. R. Leavis and C. P. Snow, Edmund Wilson and Vladimir Nabokov, and William F. Buckley and Gore Vidal, to name only a few. From the story he tells it would appear that backbiting, slander, and outright bigotry ("I dislike his face, and his manner, and his work," said Samuel Butler of Dante Gabriel Rosetti, "and I hate his poetry and his friends"), as well as real disagreements over real issues, have been part of the Western literary scene from the very beginning.[1]

Japan, too, has had its share of such disputes. One of the most recent and best known occurred between the novelists Tanizaki Jun'ichirō and Akutagawa Ryūnosuke in the late 1920s over the question of the ultimate artistic value of plot in fiction.[2] So abstract (and, in all, polite) were the arguments between the men, however, that one can find little in their correspondence to compare with their Western counterparts in viciousness and wit. One must look to Mushanokoji Saneatsu, a contemporary of both novelists, for a wicked phrase, namely, his characterization of Tanizaki as a writer "with a thought-content of zero" (*shisōteki na mono wa mattaku zero*).[3] Defenders of Tanizaki can find consolation by reminding themselves that, thoughtful or not, their mentor is now considered a major novelist worldwide, whereas the name Mushanokoji Saneatsu is remembered today only by his family, a few literature professors, and the poor school children who are forced to read his saccharine essays.

The most celebrated literary dispute in Japanese history, however, did not occur in the twentieth century, or in the age of Dr. Johnson, or even in the age of Shakespeare, but much earlier, in the late Kamakura and Muromachi periods (1250–1500); and it was not a dispute that is remembered now for the humorous quips it left to literary history, but for the profound impact it had upon the whole future course of Japanese poetry.

As might be expected in the setting of medieval Japan, the dispute began as a quarrel over inheritance, this one between two sons of Fujiwara no Tameie (1198–1275), himself a son of the great Fujiwara no Teika (1162–1241) and a grandson of Fujiwara no Shunzei (1114–1204). As heir of the Mikohidari house, whose status at court was virtually dependent on the literary activities of its heir, Tameie was expected to devote himself to poetry, which he did, acting as contest judge and critic at court and producing some competent although not particularly inspired poetry in the process. In his later years, however, his peace was disturbed by conflicts between his designated heir, Tameuji (1222–1286), and his own second wife, Ankamon'in no Shijō (generally known now as the Nun Abutsu, d. 1282), a strong and very astute woman who was anxious to protect the interests of her infant son, Tamesuke (1263–1328). For himself, Tameie too seems to have had great affection for the son of his old age. At the urging of the boy's mother, he even went so far as to will to Tamesuke several important estate rights previously given to Tameuji, along with a treasure trove of literary documents that represented the true wealth of the Mikohidari family. In this way the stage was set for what was to become one of the longest and most all-encompassing literary disputes in world history.

The real trouble began after Tameie's death, when Tameuji

went to court in an attempt to have his estate rights and the family poetic documents restored to his care. In the beginning, he triumphed by virtue of his strong backing in Kyōto; but Tamesuke's mother brought a countersuit, and thus the conflict continued, creating a rift in the house that was never again to be repaired. And another breach, this one even wider, developed when another of Tameie's sons, Tamenori (1226–1279), decided early on to defy the main house and support his young half-brother. Thus the three branches of the Mikohidari house were born: the Nijō, descending from Tameuji; the Kyōgoku, descending from Tamenori; and the Reizei, descending from Tamesuke.[4]

In time, this conflict among Tameie's sons reached out to involve nearly all late medieval poets, who, in a literary world that regarded the transmission of "secret teachings" (*denju*) from master to disciple as the only legitimate entrée into its precincts, could not avoid becoming identified with one faction or the other. Both sides—the one comprising the main house and its supporters, and the other the heirs and allies of the Kyōgoku and Reizei lines—sought support for their viewpoints in the imperial chambers, where they found, quite by chance, a division that resembled their own. Why the various parties ended up in the configuration they did is a complex story; suffice it to say that in the end, the Nijō gained the backing of the Daikakuji line of emperors, and the Kyōgoku-Reizei attracted the interests of the rival line, known as the Jimyō-In. With such powerful patrons, both factions were able to extend their rivalry into the future for generations to come.

It was at the beginning that the conflict was the most fierce, and the most public. The central literary event around which the combatants gathered was usually the commissioning of an imperial collection of poetry—precisely the sort of event that had been the center of more minor disputes for the past several centuries. In general, the Nijō line prevailed, winning for itself the honor of compiling eight such works, beginning with the *Shoku shūishū* (Collection of Gleanings Continued) in 1278 and ending with the last imperial collection, *Shin zokukokinshū* (New Collection of Ancient and Modern Times Continued) in 1439. Only twice, with the *Gyokuyōshū* (Collection of Jeweled Leaves, 1313) and the *Fūgashū* (Collection of Elegance, 1346), were the Kyōgoku and Reizei families so fortunate—mostly because of their affiliation with the ill-fated Jimyō-In emperors in the early days and later because of the dominance of the Nijō house in a society that often valued bloodline and social position more than poetic talent.

Yet the political dimensions of the conflict should not be allowed to obscure the real stylistic and philosophical disagreements between the rival houses. Broadly speaking, one may say that the Nijō poets (meaning both heirs of that family and their students and supporters) adopted a cautious, conservative, and generally idealistic approach to their art, while their cousins in the Kyōgoku-Reizei camp tended to be more open and liberal in their habits, and to champion the cause of realism. In order to obtain a more concrete notion of their differences, however, one must look to their critical and polemical writings and to the poems themselves.

One of the earliest and most significant of Nijō treatises is *Waka Teikin* (A Primer for Poets, 1326), a short cautionary piece written by Nijō Tameyo (1250–1338). As is typical of such works, it is cast in the format of a teacher instructing his pupil and covers a list of topics involving such important concepts as *kokoro* (theme, conception, meaning, and so on) and *kotoba* (diction, imagery, rhetoric, and so on). The substance of its pronouncements may be paraphrased in this way:

On the notion of seeking the new in kokoro:

This is something the ancients taught, and so do we. But to achieve newness in kokoro is not easy, and it must not be allowed to lead one toward vulgarity in theme or conception. Only poems of deep, proper feeling and beautiful conception can be called truly fine.

On the notion of favoring the old in kotoba:

Again, this is something the old masters taught, as do we. But too many poets these days do not know what the phrase *kotoba wa furuki* really means. It does not mean that we should use the more indecorous words of the *Man'yōshū* [mid-eighth century], or even of the *Kokinshū* [ca. 905], *Gosenshū* [ca. 951], and *Shūishū* [ca. 1006]. Nor should we use obscure words with which no one is familiar. To compose with gentle, mellifluous words is the way of the truly skillful poet.

On the matter of yojō:

The more skillful a poet becomes, the more his work will display *yojō*— overtones that go beyond the words to the heart. The goal of poetry should be to convey great feeling in a few short lines; bad poems do the opposite—they convey too little feeling with a superfluity of words.

On carefully pondering poetic topics [dai]:

In composing on conventional topics, one should adhere to the basic definitions arrived at in the past. Topics such as "young sprouts," "warbler," "blossoms," and "wisteria" should not be treated in the style of loneliness [sabi]; since summer comes after the blossoms have fallen and the birds have gone north, there should be no attempt to bring coolness to the green growth of the trees. Nor should one offend against the basic nature of a topic, putting a word like "dawn" in a poem on "leaves falling in the evening."

On allusion to foundation poems [honka]:

> When alluding to poems from the *Man'yōshū* that may include inappropriate vocabulary, one should refer only to the kokoro of the poem, without borrowing any of its kotoba. And one should not allude to obscure poems that people are unlikely to know.[5]

Thus the poets of the conservative camp founded their approach less in the teachings of Teika—who in his own time had been accused of the same sorts of offenses as those noted by Tameyo[6]—than in equivocations on the same: "refinements" that stress decorousness in theme, orthodoxy in vocabulary and syntax, and adherence to courtly definitions of topics and themes. Other Nijō treatises used other metaphors and examples to establish their arguments, but few departed from Tameyo's basic philosophy.

For a characterization of the unorthodox approach, one may turn to another Nijō work, *Nomori no kagami* (The Fieldguard's Mirror, 1295?), which contains the most pithy attacks on the opponents of the conservative camp. Specifically, the assault is aimed at the iconoclastic poet-critic Kyōgoku Tamekane (1254–1332).

> Tamekane teaches that one should express one's feelings directly, just as one likes; instead of adorning his feelings with words, he composes as if he were writing prose.[7]

Tamekane would of course have been annoyed with the tone of this characterization, and perhaps with the accusation that his poems differed little from prose.[8] But he would almost certainly have sanctioned the idea of direct expression; and his work—by design—does indeed break the Nijō rule of treating words as no more than a medium for fine courtly sentiments. His whole philosophy was based on the notion that words could create a direct representation of the world "as experienced."

Unfortunately, the only critical work Tamekane produced was written in his thirties, well before the poetic works of the *Gyokuyōshū* that made him famous.[9] But even in this early articulation of his approach he makes two things abundantly clear: first, that for him poetry was nothing if not an honest representation of the poet's feelings, whether those feelings were deemed appropriate by traditional conventions or not; and second, that the best poetic work emerged from direct observation of nature, rather than through the mediation of traditional themes, images, and concepts. Thus, whereas Nijō poet looked at a landscape and then wrote not so much about what *was* there as what *ought* to be there, based on poetic ideals, Tamekane and his group restricted themselves to careful perception of what the natural world presented on its own terms (*ari no mama*).

In most other ways, too, the unorthodox poets refused to be bound by Nijō idealism. In kokoro, they championed sincere reaction—although still courtly reaction, reflecting a heightened aesthetic sensibility clearly beyond the capability of the common man to achieve —regardless of the presence or absence of precedents in the poems of the past; in kotoba, they freely used the interdicted words of the *Man'yōshū* and other words of a "vulgar" nature, claiming that no word, no syntax, no imagery should be judged inappropriate except in poetic context; and in their treatment of dai, poetic topics, they allowed themselves the freedom to be as original as the occasion might demand. In all things, they were open, free-spirited, and defiant of the narrow mores of Tameyo and his salon, whom they considered stuffy and alienated from real human experience.[10]

In practice, this meant that the poets memorialized in the *Gyokuyōshū* and *Fūgashū* showed careful attention to the raw data of the natural world—the feel of the wind on the skin, the subtle shifts in color from dawn to dusk, the movements of light and shadow. Often, as in the following example by Tamekane, their poems seem to push the perceiver into the background, letting the impressions of a scene almost speak for themselves:

> Out on the waves
>   the last rays of the evening sun
>   shimmer for a moment,
> but that far little island
>   is already in darkness.[11]

In its reliance on a conception strictly mediated through poetic convention in the form of a stock metaphor *(kasumi no seki,* "gate of spring mist") handled much as it been handled in ages past, a poem by Tameyo provides a clear contrast to the Kyōgoku style:

> Could I but have my way,
> I would place it in the sky—
> that gate of spring haze.
> There at least it might forestall
>   the geese on their cloudy way.[12]

Putting the matter another way, one may say that Tamekane's poem is cinematic—a landscape, albeit one suffused with subtle movements; whereas Tameyo's is cerebral, representing an elegant idea infused less with direct perception than with the deep feeling *(ushin)* that was at the heart of Nijō poetics. Both are impressionistic in that they record the effect of a scene on the poet; and each is a fine poem in its own way. But the difference in approaches could hardly be more obvious—to readers today as well as to the poets of the late Kamakura age who were asked to choose between the competing styles.

It is in poetry of natural description that the contrasts between the two styles appear in most clear relief. But in the other major category of the court salons—love poetry—the differences can be observed as well. For instance, a poem by Emperor Fushimi (1265–1317), great patron of Tamekane's cause, reveals his belief in honest, forthright expression:

> Come to me tonight—
> and if all your promises
> on nights to come
> should turn out to be lies,
> then let them be lies.[13]

Another poem by Tameyo approaches the same basic topic in another way, a way more quaint, perhaps, but for that very reason less forceful, and—from the Kyōgoku point of view—less convincing as a statement of real emotion:

> What use is prayer
> if the one I pray about
>   remains so heartless?
> Were my prayers not answered
> I would only resent the gods.[14]

Once again, defenses for either poem can be made; the major difference between the two is less one of material than of approach, Emperor Fushimi adopting a more direct, passionate mode of expression and Tameyo relying on an a witty circumlocution to represent his sentiments.

Political difficulties sent Tamekane into exile (for the second time) in 1316; and when he died, still away from the capital, in 1332, his family line came to an end, leaving his disciples in the Jimyō-In imperial house and a few Reizei adherents to carry on the alternative tradition. Thus only for very brief periods were the champions of experience "as it is" able to truly dominate the poetic life of the capital. Instead, the Nijō family and its supporters, particularly the priest-poet Tonna (1289–1372), set the standards of court poetry for the next half century. A few less orthodox poets—most notably Reizei Tamehide (1302–1372)—

managed to make a name for themselves despite the dominant position of the Nijō family, but Tamekane's brand of experimentation was almost altogether abandoned in favor of a bland style that only occasionally produced good poetry. Nijō critical writings of the age show little departure from Tameyo's standards. And in their few references to Tamekane, his work is designated as the *ifū* ("warped style") of a misguided coterie.

But all things come to those who persevere. And in the early years of the fifteenth century, the unorthodox cause found a final champion in Imagawa Ryōshun (1326–1420), a warrior who devoted much of his time even during military campaigns to the Way of Poetry. There being no Kyōgoku heirs left to support, he chose to defend the reputation of the Reizei house—by all accounts a less strident and creative tradition than Tamekane's, but one committed nonetheless to the ideas of realism and direct expression. Vilifying Tonna and his descendants as impostors and charlatans, he put forward Reizei Tamemasa (1361–1417), the son and heir of Tamehide and his own teacher, as the only legitimate heir of Teika—and with some success. With the backing of the Ashikaga shōgun Yoshimochi (1386–1428), the Reizei heir was made a Major Counselor; he was the only one of his family ever to receive the post that had become the birthright of the main representative of the Mikohidari house. He may have been named Major Counselor partly because the Nijō bloodline had died out by Tamemasa's day, leaving the onus of conservative leadership with another court family, the Asukai; but the freshness of Tamemasa's poems cannot be discounted as another factor in his advancement.

The more discerning poets of the fifteenth century, however, were soon to see what one can only call the bankruptcy of the unorthodox *and* the conservative traditions—both of which were by that time interested primarily in preserving their own territories at court. Such a poet was Shōtetsu (1381–1459), a disciple of Ryōshun who went on to become the last great innovator of the court tradition. In the 1420s and 1430s he carried on in his teacher's place as a defender of Reizei fortunes, but in his last decades he turned back to the source of the whole medieval tradition—Teika and the poets of the Shinkokin age—for his inspiration:

It may be true that I am the heir of Tamehide and Ryōshun, but in my poetry I seek only for the deep secrets of Teika and Jichin. For those degenerate houses of latter days— the Nijō and the Reizei—I have no real attachments.[15]

One may argue that, whatever his critical stance, Shōtetsu composed his poetry according to ideals more consistent with the Kyōgoku-Reizei approach than with the Nijō. But even in his characterizations of those philosophies he hearkened back to Teika for his authority, as a short anecdote in the hand of a contemporary makes clear:

On the first day of the Fourth Lunar month, 2nd year of the Hōtoku era [1450], I paid my first visit of the year to Shōtetsu's hut. We chatted about this and that, and he said this about the Nijō and Reizei styles:

The poets of the Nijō house tend toward this kind of poem:

Off at Tatsuta,
white clouds form layers on the hills
as spring begins:
the ridges of Mount Ogura
seem to glow with cherry blossoms!

The Reizei did not compose in just one style. But most basic for them is a poem such as this:

Scattered all about,
they cannot catch the colors

of the blossoming grasses—
dewdrops carried on the wind
over the Miyagi Moors.[16]

Needless to say, both the poems are by Teika.[17] And they are well chosen to represent contrasting styles, the first one based on a panoramic view of an *utamakura* (famous place), Ogura Mountain in Tatsuta, and the second a more close-up description of dew at the mercy of the wind on the Miyagi Moors. But Shōtetsu's choice of poems was no doubt also meant to convey another truth about Teika; namely, that he was the source of both the Nijō and Kyōgoku-Reizei styles in the very beginning.

His point is worth stressing for what it reveals about the Nijō vs. Kyōgoku-Reizei dispute. Since the days of Tameuji, Nijō poets had favored the Teika of the *Shin chokusenshū* (New Imperial Collection, 1234), an imperial anthology compiled late in his life that was thought to be a model for those seeking the subtle tones of his mature ushin style; and in practice they had also recommended *Shoku gosenshū* (Later Collection Continued, 1251), an anthology compiled by Tameie. And why? Primarily because the later Teika and Tameie were safe, if somewhat staid, models for all poets—something that could not be said for all poets of the past, especially those of the *Shin kokinshū* (New Collection of Ancient and Modern Times), long held to represent the golden age of Japanese poetry. Nijō Yoshimoto (1320–1388), a man who began his career in the unorthodox camp but ended it as a conservative, states the gist of the matter in admirably direct terms: "There is no collection so interesting as the *Shin kokinshū*. But it is a bad model for the inexperienced."[18]

The conservatives were thus conservatives in the textbook sense of the term: men intimidated by experimentation and threatened by change, who advocated the plain style because it allowed even the inexperienced to gain a measure of poetic excellence—meaning usually the excellence of craftsmen, not of creative artists.

Yoshimoto cautiously goes on to say that there can be no harm in a true master's perusal of the poems of the golden age; but several lines later he quotes Tonna as saying that no poet of the present day can ever match the accomplishments of the past—implying, perhaps, that it would be best not to try.[19]

The Kyōgoku-Reizei poets, in the beginning, at least, felt quite differently. Instead of the wizened Teika of Nijō legend, they favored the stylistic firebrand of the *Shin kokinshū*, the younger Teika who had dared to experiment in both kokoro and kotoba, and in so doing had created some of the most brilliant poems his culture was ever to produce. Such an approach involved more risk, of course; but one could claim, rightly, that the results were often truly outstanding. That those who advocated such a project were destined to be in the minority seems only natural, in retrospect. The rate of worldly success among artistic adventurers has never been very high. Thus the literary history of the years 1250–1500 is dominated by Nijō poets and Nijō poetic anthologies, but always with a few Kyōgoku-Reizei dissenters thrown in, without whose influence—for they did influence some of their rivals in the conservative ranks, if almost against their will—the story of the medieval uta might have been a ponderous one indeed.

Clearly, Shōtetsu too favored in most ways the younger Teika, whose breadth allowed for a number of different styles—a major tenet of Ryōshun and the whole Reizei camp.[20] And this meant that to the extent that the Reizei family of his day represented a truly liberating force, he supported it. Above all, what he seems to have wanted was the freedom to follow his own sources of inspiration and escape the identity imposed on those who were thought of as representatives of schools or factions. His worship of Teika—and of his whole work, not just selected parts of it—may be taken as an attempt to rise above the petty disputes of his time.

Shōtetsu's near-disavowal of the Nijō and Reizei camps, both of which he correctly saw as trapped within their own traditions, amounted to a kind of prescience; for not long after his own death, court civilization and nearly everything that went with it went up in the flames of the Ōnin War (1467–1477). Although his own students carried his tradition on for a time, they also carried it mostly away from the court, to the halls of provincial war barons. A few of them were in fact not legitimate court poets at all, but masters of linked verse *(renga)* who were to bring the new vitality of their genre to the world of the uta, albeit for only a short time. By the turn of the next century a truly new genre— *haikai renga,* or "light linked verse"—was beginning to dominate Japanese poetry, attracting the finest poetic talent of a new age.

So the age-old dispute came to its end, after nearly two hundred and fifty years. And what effect had it had on literary history? The cynic's answer is that it had the profoundly negative effect of muddling good artistic minds with issues that were not really issues, political or otherwise—as well as keeping most of those minds closed to truly new and different ways of expression. But no genre can be separated from its historical context, least of all a genre that would never have existed at all without imperial and aristocratic patronage and the political entanglements such patronage inevitably involved. One must finally take a tradition for what it is, not what it could have been. Like other literary disputes in other times and places, the battles between Nijō and Kyōgoku-Reizei poets had the primary effect of focusing literary minds on issues that seemed of importance at the time. Beyond that, one can only say that the long-running dispute between the cousins of the Mikohidari house gave structure to literary history as it was happening, and it continues to do so for scholars studying the late medieval period today. One can perhaps talk about Henry James without mentioning his tendentious attacks on H. G. Wells; but no student of late medieval uta can begin his study of a poet of that era without first situating him in relation to the camps of Tamekane and Tameyo.

In the end, however, the most important bequest of the dispute is the poems themselves—for both the conservatives and their opponents produced some fine poetry, nearly all of which has been neglected by chroniclers of Japanese poetic history. In it one will find little of the wittiness of the *Kokinshū* and only a measure of the rhetorical brilliance of the *Shinkokinshū*. But even the most conservative of Nijō poets occasionally created work of resonance and subtle emotional power; and the Kyōgoku poets, with their impressionistic landscapes and straightforward love poems, in many ways prefigure the great *haikai* poets Matsuo Bashō (1644–1694) and Yosa Buson (1716–1783).

In the following pages, the reader will find just over four hundred poems, all in the thirty-one-syllable uta form. Thirty-six poets are represented, the first being Teika—who is included, along with his contemporary Ietaka, as the forerunner of all that was to come in the late medieval period—and the last being Sanjōnishi Sanetaka (1455–1537). That thirty-two of the poets included are men is a reflection of the social realities of the medieval period, especially of a shift, beginning even in Kamakura days, from the court as the center of literary activity to the cells of clerics and the halls of the warrior class. All of the major poets of both sides of the dispute have been included, although not in equal proportions.

In my selection of poems I have been influenced by practical matters such as the availability of commentaries, indexes, and other helps; otherwise, I have been guided only by a desire to show each poet at his best, trusting that in the end a reasonably clear distinction between the conservative and liberal approaches will appear. If more poems from the unorthodox poets have been included than their place in literary history seems to warrant, it is partly because more poems are needed to represent the variety of their styles, and partly because I believe that the best of them represent the most interesting poetry the age has to offer.

My approach to translation has been a very pragmatic one. In general, I have attempted to maintain a schema roughly resembling the rhythm that pertains in the originals themselves, with the syllable-count of 5-7-5-7-7 in the Japanese being suggested by my five-line format. I have also tried to indicate the variety of stops, pauses, and hesitations encountered in the originals by using a variety of indentations.

In my approach to the "meanings" of the poems, I have tried to exercise the sort of restraint that is one of the chief virtues of the works themselves. Inevitably, I have at times been forced to give in to an openly interpretive rendering, as opposed to the more implicitly interpretive rendering any translation entails; but, in general, I have tried to avoid making overly explicit in my English versions what is left to the power of suggestion in Japanese. Finally, I will admit to having consciously stayed away from poems that involved difficult wordplay or punning that simply could not be made over into English. My only defense in this is to say that such rhetorical features are less important in medieval poetry than, say, in the poetry of the early classical period—except in the cases of Teika and Shōtetsu, whose originals are at times too rhetorically complex for any translator to adequately reflect in any case.

Each poet is introduced with a short biographical sketch that attempts to place him or her in historical context and to provide a few words of critical evaluation, based generally on comments made in medieval treatises and critiques. Chapter groupings are made primarily to give structure to the book, and not to suggest any clear parallels in the "periods" of literary history, which exist only in retrospect.

NOTES

1. See Land 1983. Samuel Butler's remark is quoted in Hanser 1966:71.
2. For details of the dispute, see Ueda 1976: 71–72, 80; and Keene 1984:575–576.
3. Quoted in Itō 1970:219.
4. For details of the dispute, see Brower 1981, and Brower and Miner 1961:345–356.
5. *NKT (Nihon kagaku taikei)* 4:115–120. For a list of abbreviations used here and elsewhere in this book, see pp. 333–335.
6. See for instance Retired Emperor Go-Toba's estimations of Teika, in Brower 1972.
7. *NKT* 4:68.
8. Iwasa 1984:70–71 argues that this accusation may have more truth in it than scholars have generally believed.
9. See Huey and Matisoff 1985 for a fine translation of this important work, with a critical introduction and many helpful notes.
10. See Iwasa 1976:10–16 for a good summary of the Kyōgoku approach.
11. GYS 2095.
12. ShokuSZS 57.
13. GYS 1390.
14. ShokuSZS 1233.
15. *Oi no kurigoto, NST* 23:417.
16. *Tōyashū kikigaki, NKT* 5:346.
17. The first is SKKS 91, the second ShokuGSS 292.
18. *Kinrai fūtei, NKT* 5:143.
19. Ibid.
20. See for instance *Ryōshun isshiden, NKT* 5:183.

Waiting for the Wind

FOUNDERS

Fujiwara no Teika

Fujiwara no Ietaka

Asukai Masatsune

Fujiwara no Teika (1162–1241)

It would be difficult to introduce Fujiwara no Teika (sometimes called Sadaie) without saying something about his father, Shunzei (or Toshinari; 1114–1204). Already a major court poet at the time of Teika's birth, Shunzei went on to become a kind of Dean of Letters for his generation. As well as being one of the first court poets to approach his art with the high seriousness of a priestly vocation, he was also a major critic, contest judge, and scholar. Along with his friend Saigyō (1118–1190), he is now regarded as among the most profound and captivating of medieval poets, whose works maintain the high elegance of earlier ages and yet still produce the depth of feeling that is at the heart of the medieval mystique. Many of the critical ideals of later generations, especially *yūgen* ("mystery and depth") and *sabi* ("loneliness"), find their first important statement in his treatises and their first artistic expression in his poems.

Shunzei had many offspring, but Teika's precocious talent made him his father's favorite from a young age. Studying under Shunzei's careful direction, Teika made rapid progress, becoming a fitting heir to Shunzei's Mikohidari house. In his twenties he was active in court salons; and by the last years of the twelfth century he had already gained a reputation—a rather bad one among conservatives—for stylistic verve and rhetorical virtuosity. In 1201 he was among the eleven poets appointed Fellows (*yoriudo*) to the Poetry Bureau of Retired Emperor Go-Toba (1180–1239); that same year he was made one of the six compilers of the *Shin kokinshū* (New Collection of Ancient and Modern Times, 1206), eighth and considered by most scholars to be the best of all the imperial waka anthologies. Forty-six of his own poems were included in that collection, many of them examples of his *yōen* style ("ethereal elegance")—a highly lyrical style compounded of great rhetorical dexterity, tonal and thematic complexity, allusive depth, and richness in language and imagery.

Despite the accomplishments of his younger years, Teika's life at court was not always an easy one. Some rivals resented his natural gifts, others were offended by his proud and irascible temperament; still others were probably put off by his obvious dedication to an art that they considered little more than an elegant pastime. His advancement in rank was slow, and only by his father's intervention was he able to remain in the good graces of his patrons. After Shunzei's death in 1204 Teika had a falling out with Go-Toba, who seems to have had doubts about his approach all along; thereafter Teika turned for support to the future Emperor Juntoku (1197–1242; r. 1210–1221), the leader of whose salon he remained until the emperor and Go-Toba were both sent into exile in 1221 for conspiracy against the Kamakura shogunate. During this time Teika wrote a number of important critical treatises, mostly for patrons in the imperial family and other high nobles.[1]

Teika never attained the official recognition enjoyed by his father. After being advanced in 1232 to the office of Provisional Middle Counselor (he held Senior Second rank at the time), he took the tonsure and retired from active life, even losing interest in formal poetry for a time. The poems he did write in his last years were more subdued than those of his youth: simpler, understated works in what he called *ushin,* the style of intense feeling. The best record of this quieter style is the *Shin chokusenshū* (New Imperial Collection) of 1234, an imperial anthology for which he was sole compiler.

Teika was respected by virtually all later poets, who looked upon him as the founding father of the medieval poetic tradition.

Predictably, however, the several branches of his heirs chose different parts of his oeuvre for special attention and praise—thus extending Teika's own confusions and inconsistencies into the future. Nijō adherents thus spoke of his early work only with caution, recommending the yōen style only for those experienced enough to use it wisely. Their approbation for the late Teika, on the other hand, was less reserved; much like the advocates of Buddhism's Greater Vehicle, they argued that it was the Teika of the *Shin chokusenshū,* of ushin and rhetorical restraint, that represented the True Law.[2] Criticizing those who continually dredged up their patriarch's unusual works as examples of excellence, they insisted that the mature Teika was the only proper role model for aspiring poets.

Advocates of a more liberal approach, including the Kyōgoku and Reizei families most of the time, were less discriminating in their appreciation of Teika's work—or so their conservative opponents were wont to say. From their own point of view, those of the liberal school were simply more open-minded. For them the Teika of the *Shin kokinshū* was more exciting and more innovative—in all, a better model for those who sought excellence in the present and not merely imitation of the past. In this sense, the liberals can be said to have understood the legacy of Teika— who as an artist was nothing if not versatile and curious—in a more complete way than their Nijō rivals. But both schools could claim Teika as a teacher with some justification. That few of them were able to match him for sheer poetic talent is one of the saddest but most inescapable facts of medieval poetic history.

NOTES

1. For Go-Toba's criticisms of Teika, see Brower 1972; fine translations of Teika's *Kindai shūka* and *Maigestushō* are available in Brower and Miner 1967 and Brower 1985, respectively.

2. Although their doctrines represented a later development in the history of Buddhism, advocates of the Greater Vehicle (*Mahayana*)—as opposed to what they called the Lesser Vehicle (*Hinayana; Theravada* was the name used by followers themselves)—claimed an all-transcending power for their tradition, which centered on the final sermons of the historical Buddha as contained in the *Lotus Sutra* and other texts.

Poems

SG 59 (WINTER) [From a hundred-poem sequence composed in 1181]

1

Anxious over blossoms,
worrying over the moon,
I let time go by—
until the days made a year
    piled up like this snow.

SG 3473 (SPRING) [From a hundred-poem sequence composed in 1182]

2

His rope broken,
the loosed colt runs free
    over the spring fields—
and yet he does not wander
    far from the cherry blossoms.

SG 188 (MISCELLANEOUS) "Night" [From a hundred-poem sequence composed in 1186]

3

As I lay awake
   with my mind lost in the past,
it must have crossed the sky.
And who knows where it will end?
—the moon with its light.

SG 397 (MISCELLANEOUS) [From a hundred-poem sequence composed in 1187]

4

The black of my hair
   is now mixed with the color
      of the driven snow—
but why should that bring a change
   to the color of my heart?

SG 705 (HEAVENLY OBJECTS*) [From a hundred-poem sequence composed in 1191]

5

Too momentary
   to be called evanescent:
by a lightning strike
   I was awakened
      from my naptime dream.

* An ancient lexical category included the sun, the moon, the stars, etc.

SG 765 (BEASTS*) [From a hundred-poem sequence composed in 1191]

6

Not a soul is left
    walking out on the streets
        of the mountain village.
The barking of a watchdog
    is the only sound.[1]

* An ancient lexical category.

SG 858 (LOVE) "Waiting for Love" [From a hundred-poem sequence
composed in 1193]

7

A cruel wind blows
    over rough-stalked bush clover*—
and on my sleeves too
    I can see the moon's decline
        in heavy beads of dew.†

* *Hagi.* A large shrub that produces tiny reddish-pink blossoms each
autumn.
† The poet sees the moon reflected in dewdrops blown onto the leaves
of the bush clover by the "cruel" wind. The "heavy beads of dew" on
his sleeves are his own tears.

SG 889 (LOVE) "Love, with Boar as an Image" [From a hundred-poem sequence composed in 1193]

> 8
> I do not complain—
> though others may rest as easy
>   as a boar in his bed:
> For my laments show my love—
> as my sleeplessness, my vows.[2]

SG 3121 [From a group of poems composed in 1196]

> 9
> With the flower brocades
>   of the emperor's chambers*
>   still in my mind,
> how sad seems my little hut
>   under passing autumn showers.[3]

* *Ransei*. Literally, the Daijōkan, or Council of State. Here used to refer to the offices of high court officials in the palace.

SG 1554 (WINTER) [From a group of poems composed in 1196]

> 10
> Listen, you who don't
>   think on the sadness of things—
> hear that wild duck
>   calling by a frozen pond
>   in a mountain village.[4]

SG 1771 (LOVE) "Love Expressed with Rain as an Image" [From a fifty-poem sequence composed in 1201]

11
The raindrops drip down—
falling where I've waited long
   beneath the long eaves,
sheltered from the watchman's eyes—
waiting for my love to come.[5]

SKKS 38 (SPRING) Among poems composed for a fifty-poem sequence requested by Cloistered Prince Shukaku [1198*]

12
On this spring night,
the floating bridge of my dreams
   has broken away:
and lifting off a far peak—
a cloudbank trails into the sky.[6]

* Here and elsewhere in this section, bracketed numbers (my interpolations) indicate date of composition. All headnote material that is not in brackets is translated from the anthologies.

13
Blossoms of plum
    perfume my sleeves with their scent,
vying there for space
    with shafts of sparkling moonlight
        spilling down through the eaves.[7]

SKKS 91 (SPRING) From a hundred-poem sequence [1200]

14
Off at Tatsuta,*
white clouds form layers on the hills
    as spring begins:
the ridges of Mount Ogura†
    seem to glow with cherry blossoms![8]

* A mountainous area just southwest of the old capital at Nara that was noted for its autumn leaves and, to a lesser extent, for its cherry blossoms.
† One of the peaks in the Tatsuta area.

> 15
> Not a trace is left
>   of that blossom-tinted wind
>   that filled my garden.
> Those who visit me now
>   will see only fallen snow.[9]

* A contest involving poems commissioned by Emperor Go-Toba, with judgments by Shunzei and others.

> 16
> Looking far, I see
>   no sign of cherry blossoms
>   or crimson leaves:
> a reed-thatched hut on a bay
>   on an evening in autumn.[10]

17
The seasonless waves
of the Izumi River*
are changing colors:
storm winds must be blowing
up in the Hahaso Groves.[11]

* An older name for the modern Kizu River, which runs through Yamashiro (modern Kyōto Municipality), with headwaters near the Hahaso Groves.

SKKS 671 (WINTER) From a hundred-poem sequence [1200]

18
No shelter in sight
to give my pony a rest
and brush off my sleeves—
in the fields around Sano Ford*
on a snowy evening.[12]

* Near Miwanosaki in Kii (modern Wakayama Prefecture).

SKKS 672 (WINTER) Written on the topic "Snow at a Mountain Home," when the Regent–Prime Minister was still a Major Counselor [1189]

19

Could it be I wait
    for one whose path is blocked
        at the foot of the hill?
The snow is weighing heavy
    on the cedars at my eaves.

SKKS 788 (PARTING) One stormy day during the autumn his mother had passed away, he went to his old home [1193]

20

For the jewel-like dew
    as for my falling tears,
there is no respite:
both scatter on the autumn wind
    at the house where one has died.[13]

SKKS 955 (TRAVEL) A Travel poem [1196]

21

With the autumn wind
    turning back the flowing sleeves
        of a traveler,
how lonely in evening light
    is the bridge up on the peak.*

* *Kakehashi.* A rope bridge spanning a mountain gorge.

SKKS 968 (TRAVEL) A Travel poem, written for a poetry contest at the
home of the Regent–Prime Minister [1200]

> 22
> I want only to forget—
> don't tell me they are waiting,
> you autumn wind
>   blowing so incessantly
>   from Inaba's* peak.[14]

* Modern Tottori Prefecture.

SKKS 1117 (LOVE) On the topic "Love, with Sea Imagery" [1187]

> 23
> A Suma* fisherman
>   may know the ring of the sea breeze
> as it hurries along
>   through his sleeves and away—
> but can he catch it in his hand?

* A rugged coastal area in Settsu, just west of modern Kōbe.

SKKS 1142 (LOVE) On the topic "Praying for Love," from a hundred-poem sequence composed at the house of the Regent–Prime Minister [1193]

24

The years have gone by,
with my prayers still unanswered —
as Hase's bell*
    signals evening from the peak,
sounding somehow far away.†

* A reference to the Hase Temple, located in Yamato (modern Nara Prefecture).
† A double entendre meaning both "distant" and "irrelevant"—since the evening bell signals no lover's tryst for the poet.

SKKS 1206 (LOVE) Written as a Love poem [1187]

25

After his tryst,
he too may be looking up
    on his way back home—
while for me the moon at dawn
    ends a night of vain waiting.

From a hundred-poem sequence composed at the
house of the Regent–Prime Minister for a poem contest [1193]

26
If he's not forgotten,
why would these sleeves he knows so well
    now be frozen so?
—as I lie awake, my bed
    covered with tears cold as frost.

SKKS 1390 (LOVE) Topic unknown

27
Those long black tresses
    that I roughly pushed aside—
now strand upon strand
    they rise into my mind's eye
        every night as I lie down.[15]

SCSS 852 (LOVE) A Love poem, written for an imperial poem contest
in the sixth year of the Kempō era [1219]

28
On Matsuo Beach*
    I wait in the pines at dusk
        for one who won't come—
and like the blazing salt mounds,†
    I too am consumed by fire.[16]

* Located on the northern tip of Awaji Island.
† Seaweed was dried and burned to extract salt from the ashes.

SCSS 1168 (MISCELLANEOUS) On "A Distant View," from a hundred-poem sequence written at the home of the Regent-Minister of the Left [1232]

> 29
> From the outer gate
>   of the stone-built palace*
>   I come every night—
> and always there, though unbidden,
> is the moon on the mountain rim.

* *Momoshiki no.* A fixed epithet for the imperial palace compound.

SHOKUGSS 292 (AUTUMN) Presented with a group of poems on Famous Places [1207]

> 30
> Scattered all about,
> they cannot catch the colors
>   of the blossoming grasses*—
> dewdrops carried on the wind
>   over the Miyagi Moors.†

* Dew is said to "give lodging to" things that are reflected in it: the moon, cherry blossoms, and so on. Here the blustery wind—always a spoiler—makes it impossible for the dew to stay put long enough to reflect the flowers on the blossoming grasses.
† A moorland in Rikuzen (modern Miyagi Prefecture), near Sendai, that was famous for its autumn grasses.

SHOKUGSS 309 (AUTUMN) Presented as one of ten poems in the second
year of the Kempō era [1214]

31

Surely autumn comes
   to places other than the shore
     of Takasago.*
Yet that stag seems to call out:
"This evening is mine alone."

* A bay in Harima (modern Hyōgo Prefecture) that was the site of a
famous Shinto shrine.

GYS 407 (SUMMER) From among his Summer poems [1196]

32

Too tired to move fast,
the plodding pull-ox raises dust
   with each slow step;
even the wind feels hot
   swirling round the summer cart.

GYS 708 (AUTUMN) On "Bamboos in the Wind, Beneath the Moon,"
from a fifty-poem sequence written for Retired Emperor Go-Toba [1201]

33

Too restless to sleep,
I am lured out by the moon—
   and along my path,
sweeping past the bamboo fence,
comes a gust of autumn wind.

GYS 847 (WINTER) From among his Winter poems [date unknown]

34
In a patch of sky
    between clusters of cloud
        appears a rainbow:
the showers have passed by
    the far mountain ridge.

GYS 2257 (MISCELLANEOUS) From among his Miscellaneous poems
[1187]

35
The familiar sound
    of a dog's rough bark
        tells you it's there:
back behind the bamboo grove—
    a string of houses.[17]

FGS 245 (SPRING) From a hundred-poem sequence [1190]

36
How senseless it was
    to resent the cherry blossoms
        just for falling.
Had they not fallen, would I
    be seeing this garden today?[18]

37

Off on Heaven's Plain*
 the waves and the sky
  are one and the same;
and there's no mountain ridge
 to receive the setting sun.

* *Ama no hara.* A conventional metaphor for the sky.

FGS 1744 (MISCELLANEOUS) On "Pines Around a Mountain Home,"
from a thirty-poem sequence [1225]

38

Will anyone look back
 and think of me, seeing it?
The pine at my eaves
 here on Mount Ogura,*
my home now for so long.

* A mountain on the western outskirts of the capital where Teika had
an estate at the time.

39

A shower passes
over cormorant boats
whose fishing fires†
vie in number with the stars
shining through gaps in the clouds.

* Men who fished at night with cormorants—large sea-ravens with banded necks that were trained to catch fish and then come back to the boat and disgorge them.
† *Kagaribi.* Fires kept burning in cauldrons on the prows of the boats to attract fish at night.

40

With wood from his door,
he's rebuilt the bridge of brush
across the ravine—
a hermit who still seems to want
a way back to the world.

41

The running water
   has lured away both blossoms
      and crimson leaves—
leaving only the mosses
   as master of the gorge.

SG 1427 "Early Autumn" [1232]

42

"Autumn has come"—
so the wind proclaims
   in the leaves on the reeds.
No one comes to visit me
   beneath the twilight sky.

SG 1446 (WINTER) "Snow" [1232]

43

To have grown old—
with the snow all around me
   I know what it means.
Not a soul comes to visit;
I have no place to go.

SG 1487 (AUTUMN) "Distant View" [1232]

44
Above crimson leaves
   blown about by gusts of wind,
the mists clear away—
and coming into open view
   is the peak of Storm Mountain.*

* Arashiyama. A mountain just west of Kyōto famous both for its cherry
blossoms and its autumn leaves.

SG 2177 (AUTUMN) Written at court, on "Moonlight on the Imperial
Courts" [date unknown]

45
I shall not forget—
that long night of frost
   on the royal steps,*
when the moon shone above clouds—
the moon I thought I knew.

* *Mihashi*. The southern steps leading into the Shishinden, main cer-
emonial building of the residential compound of the imperial palace.

NOTES

1. A possible allusion to a scene in the "A Boat Upon the Waters"
chapter of *The Tale of Genji*, in which Niou makes a clandestine visit to
Ukifune at Uji and finds the place being watched over by Kaoru's guards
and watchdogs. See Seidensticker 1976, 2:1007–1008.

2. An allusive variation on GSIS 821, by Izumi Shikibu (fl. ca. 970–1030) [Headnote: Topic unknown]: "Scratching at reeds, the boar makes himself a bed / and rests easy there. I will not sleep as well— / though I wish it were not so!" (*Karu mo kaki / fusu i no toko no / i o yasuku / sa koso nezarame / kakarazu mogana.*)

3. An allusion to WRS 555, by the Chinese poet Bo Juyi (772–846), which he sent to a friend in the Tang capital when he was in exile near Lu-Shan in Jiang-zi: "In the Hall of State it is blossom time—where you sit beneath curtains of brocade; / But on Lu-Shan it is raining tonight—where I sit inside a hut of grass."

4. An echo of SKKS 299, by Monk Saigyō [Headnote: Topic Unknown]: "It creates a heart / even in those among us / who think of themselves / as indifferent to all things— / this first wind of autumn." (*Oshinabete / mono o omowanu / hito ni sae / kokoro o tsukuru / aki no hatsukaze.*)

5. A possible allusion to a poem by Kaoru from "The Eastern Cottage" chapter of *The Tale of Genji* in which he complains to Ukifune about being kept waiting "so long in the rain at the eaves." See Seidensticker 1976, 2:966.

6. An allusion to the final chapter of *The Tale of Genji*, entitled "The Floating Bridge of Dreams," which leaves the fate of Ukifune as uncertain as Teika's cloud trailing off into the empty sky. See Seidensticker 1976, 2:1081–1090.

7. An allusion to KKS 747, by Ariwara no Narihira (825–880), in which the poet laments the loss of a love when visiting the house—now abandoned and run-down—where the two had met the year before: "Is this not the moon? / And is this not the springtime, / the springtime of old? / Only this body of mine / the same body as before." (*Tsuki ya aranu / haru ya mukashi no / haru naranu / waga mi hitotsu wa / moto no mi ni shite.*) McCullough 1985:165.

8. An allusion to MYS 1747, a *chōka* (long poem) by Takahashi Mushimaro (eight century): "In Tatsuta's hills, / where white clouds ever trail, / above the cascade / on the peak of Ogura, / the cherry blossoms / are blooming everywhere. . . ." (*Shirakumo no / tatsuta no yama o / taki no ue no / ogura no mine ni / sakiōru / sakura no hana wa. . . .*

9. An allusive variation on a famous exchange of poems (KKS 62 and 63) between Ariwara no Narihira and a lady [Headnote: Composed when someone called during the height of the cherry-blossom season after having stayed away a long time]: "They are called fickle, / these blossoms of the cherry, / yet they have waited / for a person whose visits / come but seldom in the year." (*Ada nari to / na ni koso tatere / sakurabana / toshi ni mare naru / hito mo machikeri.*) [Reply]: "Had I not come today, / they would have fallen tomorrow / like drifting snowflakes. / Though they have not yet melted / they are scarcely true

flowers." (*Kyō kozu wa / asu wa yuki to zo / furinamashi / kiezu wa ari tomo / hana to mimashi ya.*) McCullough 1985:25–26.

10. An allusion to descriptions of the stark scenery confronted by the exiled Genji in the "Akashi" chapter of *The Tale of Genji*. See Seidensticker 1976, 1:252, 255.

11. An allusive variation on KKS 250, by Fun'ya no Yasuhide (ninth century) [Headnote: A poem from the contest at Prince Koresada's house]: "Though each grass and tree / takes on a different hue, / there is no autumn / for the flowers blossoming / on the billows of the sea." (*Kusa mo ki mo / iro kawaredomo / watatsuumi no / nami no hana ni zo / aki nakarikeru.*) McCullough 1985:63.

12. An allusion to MYS 265, by Naga Okimaro (seventh century): "Ah, how hard it is, / to be caught in this driving rain / —for at Miwa Point / in the fields around Sano Ford / there's no house to be found." (*Kurushiki mo / furikuru ame ka / miwanosaki / sano no watari ni / ie mo aranaku ni.*)

13. Allusions to SKKS 372, by Lady Sagami (early eleventh century) [Headnote: Topic unknown]: "The dew at dawn / continues on, ceasing no more / than my falling tears; / and still there too is the sound / of the mournful wind" (*Akatsuki no / tsuyu wa namida mo / todomarazu / uramuru kaze no / koe zo nokoreru*); and to a Chinese poem by Minamoto no Tamenori (d. 1011) from *Shinsen rōeishū*: "With my mother back home, I shed tears in the autumn wind; / With not another soul here at my inn, my spirit wanders in evening rain." See Kubota 1985, 1:442.

14. An allusion to KKS 365, by Ariwara no Yukihira (818–893) [Headnote: Topic unknown]: "I must leave you now, / to journey to Inaba / where pines top the peaks, / but I will return at once / if you say you pine for me." (*Tachiwakare / inaba no yama no / mine ni ouru / matsu to shi kikeba / ima kaerikomu.*) McCullough 1985:88.

15. An allusive variation on GSIS 755, by Izumi Shikibu [Headnote: Topic unknown]: "With not a thought / for my black hair's disarray, / I lay myself down— / soon longing for the one whose hands / used to brush it smooth." (*Kurogami no / midare mo shirazu / uchifuseba / mazu kakiyarishi / hito zo koishiki.*)

16. An allusion to MYS 935, by Kasa no Kanamura (fl. 715–733), the relevant lines of which are: "At Awaji Isle, / on the Bay at Matsuho, / they cut jeweled seaweed / on the beach at morn; / they burn seaweed for salt, / on the beach at eve. . . ." (*Awajishima / matsuho no ura ni / asanagi ni / tamamo karitsutsu / yūnagi ni / moshio yakitsutsu. . . .*).

17. Another possible allusion to the "A Boat Upon the Waters" chapter of *The Tale of Genji*. See note 1 above.

18. Another allusion to KKS 62–63, by Ariwara no Narihira. See note 8 above.

JAPANESE TEXTS

1 Hana o machi / tsuki o oshimu to / sugushikite / yuki ni zo tsumoru / toshi wa shiraruru
2 Tsuna taete / arenishi koma zo / haru no no no / hana no atari wa / hanarezarikeru
3 Mukashi omou / nezame no sora ni / sugikiken / yukue mo shiranu / tsuki no hikari no
4 Kurokami wa / majirishi yuki no / iro nagara / kokoro no iro wa / kawari ya wa suru
5 Hakanashi to / miru hodo mo nashi / inazuma no / hikari ni samuru / utatane no yume
6 Yamazato wa / hito no kayoeru / ato mo nashi / yado moru inu no / koe bakari shite
7 Kaze tsuraki / motoara no kohagi / sode ni mite / fukeyuku tsuki ni / omoru shiratsuyu
8 Urayamazu / fusu i no toko wa / yasuku to mo / nageki mo katami / nenu mo chigiri o
9 Ransei no / hana no nishiki no / omokage ni / iori kanashiki / aki no murasame
10 Mono omowanu / hito no kike kashi / yamazato no / kōreru ike ni / hitori naku oshi
11 Ama sosogi / hodo furu noki no / itabisashi / hisashi ya hitome / moru to mo seshi ma ni
12 Haru no yo no / yume no ukihashi / todaeshite / mine ni wakaruru / yokogumo no sora
13 Ume no hana / nioi o utsusu / sode no ue ni / noki moru tsuki no / kage zo arasou
14 Shirakumo no / haru wa kasanete / tatsuta yama / ogura no mine ni / hana niou rashi
15 Sakurairo no / niwa no harukaze / ato mo nashi / towaba zo hito no / yuki to dani mimu
16 Miwataseba / hana mo momiji mo / nakarikeri / ura no tomaya no / aki no yūgure
17 Toki wakanu / nami sae iro ni / izumigawa / hahaso no mori ni / arashi fuku rashi
18 Koma tomete / sode uchiharau / kage mo nashi / sano no watari no / yuki no yūgure
19 Matsu hito no / fumoto no michi wa / taenuran / nokiba no sugi ni / yuki omoru nari
20 Tamayura no / tsuyu mo namida mo / todomarazu / naki hito kouru / yado no akikaze

21 Tabibito no / sode fukikaesu / akikaze ni / yūbe sabishiki / yama no kakehashi

22 Wasurenamu / matsu to na tsuge so / nakanaka ni / inaba no yama no / mine no akikaze

23 Suma no ama no / sode ni fukikosu / shiokaze no / naru to wa suredo / te ni mo tamarazu

24 Toshi mo henu / inoru chigiri wa / hatsuse yama / onoe no kane no / yoso no yūgure

25 Kaerusa no / mono to ya hito no / nagamuramu / matsu yo nagara no / ariake no tsuki

26 Wasurezu wa / nareshi sode mo ya / kōruramu / nenu yo no toko no / shimo no samushiro

27 Kakiyarishi / sono kurokami no / suji goto ni / uchifusu hodo wa / omokage zo tatsu

28 Konu hito o / matsuo no ura no / yūnagi ni / yaku ya moshio no / mi mo kogaretsutsu

29 Momoshiki no / tonoe o izuru / yoi yoi wa / matanu ni mukau / yama no ha no tsuki

30 Utsuriaenu / hana no chigusa ni / midaretsutsu / kaze no ue naru / miyagino no tsuyu

31 Takasago no / hoka ni mo aki wa / aru mono o / waga yūgure to / shika wa naku nari

32 Yukinayamu / ushi no ayumi ni / tatsu chiri no / kaze sae atsuki / natsu no oguruma

33 Fushiwabite / tsuki ni ukaruru / michinobe no / kakine no take o / harau akikaze

34 Murakumo no / taema no sora no / niji tachite / shigure suginuru / ochi no yama no ha

35 Satobitaru / inu no koe ni zo / shirarekeru / take yori oku no / hito no iei wa

36 Chirinu tote / nadote sakura o / uramiken / chirazu wa mimashi / kyō no niwa ka wa

37 Wata no hara / nami to sora to wa / hitotsu nite / irihi o ukuru / yama no ha mo nashi

38 Shinobaremu / mono to wa nashi ni / ogurayama / nokiba no matsu zo / narete hisashiki

39 Ukaibune / murasame suguru / kagaribi ni / kumoma no hoshi no / kage zo arasou

40 Take no to no / tani no shibahashi / aratamete / nao yo o wataru / michi shitaurashi

41 Yuku mizu ni / hana mo momiji mo / sasowarete / koke koso tani no / aruji narikere

42 Aki kinu to / ogi no hakaze wa / nanoru nari / hito koso towane /
    tasogare no sora
43 Oiraku wa / yuki no uchi ni zo / omoishiru / tou hito mo nashi /
    yuku kata mo nashi
44 Fukiharau / momiji no ue no / kiri harete / mine tashika naru / ar-
    ashiyama kana
45 Wasurezu yo / mihashi no shimo no / nagaki yo ni / nareshinagara
    no / kumo no ue no tsuki

Fujiwara no Ietaka (1158–1237)

Teika was one of an extraordinary generation of poets that included Emperor Go-Toba, Princess Shikishi (d. 1201), the Regent Kujō Yoshitsune (1169–1206), the Tendai Archbishop Jien (d. 1225), and many others. But among these, Teika in his last years seems to have esteemed most of all his cousin, Ietaka, another student of Shunzei.

The son of another minor branch of the Fujiwara, Ietaka went through the usual appointments, all to relatively minor posts, gaining Junior Second rank only late in life. Like Teika, he was a member of Retired Emperor Go-Toba's salon and served as a Fellow of the Poetry Bureau in 1201 and as one of the six compilers of the *Shin kokinshu*. While dismissing the works of his younger days, Go-Toba singled Ietaka out for special praise as one whose poems displayed "noble dignity" (*take ari*) and "originality of invention" (*mezurashi*; see Brower 1972:37). If somewhat less imaginative and certainly less innovative than Teika, he was nearly the latter's equal in mastery of idiom and imagery.

In many ways, then, Ietaka was a more appropriate model for young court poets than Teika—an opinion given force by his strong representation (forty-three poems, more than any other poet) in *Shin chokusenshū*, the ninth imperial waka anthology, which, as mentioned before, was compiled by Teika's own hand in the mid-1230s. For this reason Ietaka was also praised highly by later poets, particularly those of the Nijō persuasion. His poems are masterful examples of the polished yet intense approach known in Teika's vocabulary as the ushin style.

Poems

From a hundred-poem sequence

1

Those cherry blossoms:
were they dream, or reality?
Gone are the white clouds
　　from the peak, leaving behind
　　　　the fickle wind of spring.[1]

Presented as part of a hundred-poem sequence

2

Yoshino River*—
with kerria† blossoming
　　all along its banks.
The cherries up on the peaks
　　will now be scattered and gone.

---

* A river running through the mountains of Yoshino, an area south of Nara that was famous for its cherry blossoms.
† *Yamabuki*. A yellow wildflower with five-petaled blossoms resembling a rose in shape.

3
And what now, cuckoo*—
after waiting for you in vain
    for so many nights?
No more will I wait, I think,
until a rain shower† passes by.[2]

* *Hototogisu*. A small bird of the cuckoo family who is notorious for granting the gift of its song—a harbinger of summer—only seldom, despite the impatience of poets.
† *Murasame*. A sudden rain shower—another sign of summer.

SKKS 246 (SUMMER) Topic unknown

4
Only this year
    has it begun to blossom.
How can it be, then,
that the scent of the wild orange*
    is one from so long ago.[3]

* *Tachibana*. Known for the beauty of its blossoms, the scent of which was believed to be a strong stimulus to the memory.

SKKS 289 (AUTUMN) From among the poems of a hundred-poem sequence

5
Only yesterday
I had thought I must visit—
now autumn's already come
to the grooves at Ikuta*
in the Land of Tsu.[4]

* A place in ancient Settsu (modern Kōbe) famous for its autumn leaves.

SKKS 389 (AUTUMN) Written on the topic "The Moon on the Water" for a contest at the Poetry Bureau

6
Ah, the Sea of Grebes!*
—where the moonlight glistening
upon the waters
makes it seem autumn has come
to flowers upon the waves.[5]

* Niho no Umi. A poetic name for Lake Biwa, located just to the northeast of the capital at Kyōto.

7
Gazing at the sky,
I grow lonely at the thought
    of those said to dwell
in the capital on the moon*
    as day breaks here below.

* The shadows on the moon were construed to be a palace in Chinese legend.

8
The lowermost leaves
    on the mountain are falling
        in evening showers:
is he drenched, to sound so forlorn?
—that lone stag, calling his mate.

9
The cries of crickets
    continue on through the night,
here at my old home.
Then, to add to my sad thoughts—
the wind blowing in the pines.[6]

SKKS 639 (WINTER) From a poetry contest at the house of the Regent–Prime Minister, on the topic "Winter Moon on the Water"

> 10
> Ah, the Bay at Shiga!*
> —where from between waves ebbing
>   into the distance
> comes the frozen countenance
>   of the moon at dawn.[7]

* Site of an ancient capital on the southwestern tip of Lake Biwa.

SKKS 939 (TRAVEL) From a fifty-poem sequence

> 11
> When the new day dawns
>   is that the mountain peak
>   I will be crossing?
> White clouds mark the end
>   of the moon's course through the sky.

SKKS 969 (TRAVEL) A Travel poem, from a hundred-poem sequence

12
With no lover's pledge,
I have spent the night through
    on Kiyomi Strand.*
Rising from the waves—
a cloud in the light of dawn.

* Kiyomigata. Coastal area in Suruga (modern Shizuoka Perfecture).

SKKS 1294 (LOVE) From *The Poem Contest in Fifteen Hundred Rounds*
[1201]*

13
Don't you remember?
Is this the final result
    of your promises?
Yesterday's clouds are gone,
replaced by cold mountain wind.†

* A contest involving poems commissioned by Emperor Go-Toba, with
judgments by Shunzei and others.
† *Yamakaze*. A cold wind that here symbolizes a lover's rejection.

Fujiwara no Ietaka   37

14

I look out today
   and see even the clouds
     buried in blossoms;
the haze cannot overcome
   the mountains of Yoshino.*

* Cherry blossoms and haze are the two most common indexes of spring in court poetry. Here the poet rejoices that the latter lacks the power to hide the former as they reach their glory on the hillsides of Yoshino in Yamato (modern Nara Prefecture).

SCSS 192 (SUMMER) Written on viewing an ornamental screen painted upon the occasion of Her Majesty's entrance into the imperial chambers

15

As day nears its end
   with a breeze rustling in the oaks
     along Nara Stream,*
the people doing ablutions†
   are the sole sign of summer.[8]

* A small "purification stream" (*mitarashigawa*) flowing by the Upper Kamo Shrine in northern Kyōto.
† Ritual washings symbolized purification from sins. Here Ietaka refers to washings undertaken on the last day of the sixth lunar month, halfway point of the year.

16
In the evening light
   what will the sight of the sky
      do to my heart?
Just the sound of fall's first wind
   has made me sad this morning.

SCSS 292 (AUTUMN) A poem written during autumn of the second year
of the Kenpō era [1214]

17
All things have an end—
and so the day tries to dawn
   with the early bell.*
But the long night lingers on
   with the moon still in the sky.

* Rung at temples each morning at around 6 A.M.

SCSS 393 (WINTER) Topic unknown

18

In my native home
   the sunrays in the garden
      darken into cold;
on scattered paulownia leaves,*
the sound of falling hail.

* *Kiri.* A deciduous tree of the figwort family with large, fan-shaped
yellow leaves that carpet the ground around the trees in autumn.

SCSS 424 (WINTER) Written as a Winter poem

19

In the broad dawn sky
   even the stars between the clouds
      shine with a chill light—
so cold is the mountain rim
   when its peaks are white with snow.

SCSS 975 (LOVE) Topic unknown

20

What am I to do?
If only I could doze off
   for but a moment!
—and find myself in a dream
   that would last the whole night through.

21
My ruminations
    are still far from exhausted
        when my long night ends—
with me giving in to sleep
    at the sound of the morning bell.

SHOKUGSIS 170 (SUMMER) A poem composed for a screen painting

22
Bring your first song
    and hurry to the capital,
O cuckoo*—
in the evergreen groves
    the pines grow old in waiting.

* *Hototoyisu.*

GSS 204 (SPRING)

23
To those who await
    only flowers as their sign,
I would show another spring:
grass pushing up through the snow
    in a mountain village.

24

To hear from others
   that the cherries are in bloom
      is not enough—
though days may pass before I go
   to the hills of Yoshino.*[9]

* A mountainous area in central Yamato (modern Nara Prefecture).

GGS 2817 (MISCELLANEOUS)

25

I awoke from sleep
   hearing a sad sound
      I had not listened for:
the voice of waves at daybreak
   breaking on the rocky shore.

GGS 2646 "Autumn"

26

Even the insects
   chirp with tear-choked voices
      as day nears its end.
And who comes to visit me?
Only the wind in the reeds.

NOTES

1. An allusive variation that combines lines from two KKS poems, 601 and 942. KKS 601, by Mibu no Tadamine (fl. ca. 900–910) [Headnote: Topic unknown]: "Parting from the peaks, / white clouds go to meet their end / in the blowing wind, / but there seems to be no end / to the coldness of your heart." (*Kaze fukeba / mine ni wakaruru / shirakumo no / taete tsurenaki / kimi ga kokoro ni*). KKS 942, anonymous [Headnote: Topic unknown]: "Might this world be real, / or might it be but a dream? / Whether it be dream / or reality I know not, / for we are here and not here." (*Yo no naka wa / yume ka utsutsu ka / utsutsu to mo / yume to mo shirazu / arite nakereba.*) McCullough 1985: 135, 207.

2. An allusive variation on SIS 848, by Kakinomoto Hitomaro (fl. ca. 680–700) [Headnote: Topic unknown]: "So many nights now / has he not come to me, / despite my longing— / that I spend more of my time / vowing not to wait than waiting." (*Tanometsutsu / konu yo amata ni / narinureba / mataji to omou zo / matsu ni masareru.*)

3. An allusion to KKS 139, anonymous. [Headnote: Topic unknown]: "Scenting the fragrance / of orange blossoms that await / the Fifth Month's coming, / I recall a perfumed sleeve / worn by someone long ago." (*Satsuki matsu / hanatachibana no / ka o kagebu / mukashi no hito no / sode no ka suru.*) McCullough 1985:41.

4. An allusion to SKS 81, by Monk Shōin (precise dates unknown) [Headnote: Sent when he was living in Tsu province upon the occasion of Ōe no Tamemoto's return to the capital after the end of the latter's appointment period]: "Were you still here, / I would ask what you thought of it— / this first autumn wind / blowing in the groves at Ikuta / in the Land of Tsu." (*Kimi sumaba / towashi mono o / tsu no kuni no / ikuta no mori no / aki no hatsukaze.*)

5. An allusive variation on KKS 250, by Fun'ya no Yasuhide. See note 11 in the section on Fujiwara no Teika in this anthology.

6. A possible allusion to either of two scenes from *The Tale of Genji:* "The Paulownia Court," in which Myōbu and Genji's grandmother share their grief over the death of the boy's mother; and / or "The Wind in the Pines," in which the Akashi Lady and her mother lament their loneliness at the Ōi villa, to which Genji has recently brought them from Akashi. See Seidensticker 1976, 1:9–10, 323.

7. An allusive variation on GSIS 419, by Monk Kaikaku (precise date unknown) [Headnote: Topic unknown]: "As the night grows late, / the waters along the shore / must be freezing over: / for ebbing into the distance / are the winds over Shiga Bay." (*Sayo fukuru / mama ni migiwa ya / kōruran / tōzakariyuku / shiga no urakaze.*)

8. An allusive variation that combines lines from GSIS 231, by Min-

amoto no Yoritsuna (d. 1079), and an anonymous poem from *The Six Volumes of Poetry* (*Kokin waka rokujō*, a large collection of poems from the classical ages used by poets as a handbook and primer). GSIS 231 [Headnote: Written on the topic of "Taking the Night Air and Feeling Like Autumn" at the home of Lord Toshituna]: "As day nears its end / with a breeze rustling oak leaves / in the summer hills, / this year once again / I feel as if it were autumn." (*Natsuyama no / nara no ha soyogu / yūgure wa / kotoshi mo aki no / kokochi koso sure.*) *Kokin waka rokujō* 118 (also SKKS 1376) [Headnote: A Love poem]: "As those around me / do their ablutions in the wind / off Nara Stream, / I am praying only / for my secret love not to end." (*Misogi suru / nara no ogawa no / kawakaze ni / inori zo wataru / shita ni taeji to.*)

9. An allusive variation on KKS 588, by Ki no Tsurayuki [Headnote: Sent to someone in Yamato]: "Until I go there, / I must continue merely / to hear from others / word of the cherry blossoms / in the hills of Yoshino." (*Koenu ma wa / yoshino no yama no / sakurabana / hitozute ni nomi / kikiwataru ka na.*) McCullough 1985:133.

JAPANESE TEXTS

1 Sakurabana / yume ka utsutsu ka / shirakumo no / taete tsunenaki / mine no harukaze

2 Yoshinogawa / kishi no yamabuki / sakinikeri / mine no sakura wa / chirihatenuran

3 Ika ni sen / konu yo amata no / hototogisu / mataji to omoeba / murasame no sora

4 Kotoshi yori / hana sakisomuru / tachibana no / ikade mukashi no / ka ni niouran

5 Kinō dani / towan to omoishi / Tsu no Kuni no / Ikuta no mori ni / aki wa kninkeri

6 Nio no umi ya / tsuki no hikari no / utsuroeba / nami no hana ni mo / aki wa miekeri

7 Nagametsutsu / omou mo sabishi / hisakata no / tsuki no miyako no / akegata no sora

8 Shitamomiji / katsu chiru yama no / yūshigure / nurete ya hitori / shika no nakuran

9 Mushi no ne mo / nagaki yo akanu / furusato ni / nao omoi sou / matsukaze zo fuku

10 Shiga no ura ya / tōzakariyuku / namima yori / kōrite izuru / ariake no tsuki

11 Akeba mata / koyubeki yama no / mine nare ya / sora yuku tsuki
    no / sue no shirakumo
12 Chigiranedo / hitoyo wa suginu / kiyomigata / nami ni wakaruru /
    akatsuki no kumo
13 Omoiideyo / taga kanegoto no / sue naran / kinō no kumo no / ato
    no yamakaze
14 Kyō mireba / kumo mo sakura ni / uzumorete / kasumikanetaru /
    Miyoshino no yama
15 Kaze soyogu / Nara no ogawa no / yūgure wa / misogi zo natsu
    no / shirushi narikeru
16 Kureyukaba / sora no keshiki mo / ika naramu / kesa dani kanashi
    / aki no hatsukaze
17 Kagiri areba / akenamu to suru / kane no oto ni / nao nagaki yo
    no / tsuki zo nokoreru
18 Furusato no / niwa no hikage mo / saekurete / kiri no ochiba ni /
    arare furu nari
19 Akewataru / kumoma no hoshi no / hikari made / yama no ha
    samushi / mine no shirayuki
20 Ika ni semu / shibashi uchinuru / hodo mogana / hitoyo bakari no
    / yume o dani mimu
21 Omou koto / mada tsukihatenu / nagaki yo no / nezame ni
    makuru / kane no oto ka no
22 Hatsukoe wa / miyako ni isoge / hototogisu / tokiwa no mori no /
    matsu wa furiniki
23 Hana o nomi / matsuramu hito ni / yamazato no / yukima no kusa
    no / haru o misebaya
24 Hitozute ni / sate to wa kikashi / sakurabana / yoshino no yama ni
    / hikazu koyu to mo
25 Nezame shite / kikanu o kikite / kanashiki wa / araisonami no / ak-
    atsuki no koe
26 Mushi no ne mo / namida tsuyukeki / yūgure o / tou mono tote
    wa / ogi no uwakaze

Asukai Masatsune (1170–1221)

In the medieval age, poetic talent could mean many things, among them a possible entrée into the highest circles for those whose family background might otherwise have excluded them from contact with the elite. Such was the case with Asukai Masatsune, heir of a minor branch of the Fujiwara family that before his time had won itself no special place in history.

Early political entanglements sent Masatsune's father into exile in Izu when the boy was still in his teens. Rather than giving up on his ambitions, however, Masatsune seized upon this opportunity to make a name for himself; soon he had attached himself to a powerful warrior baron in nearby Kamakura who was like himself an avid devotee of court kickball (*kemari*). After the establishment of the Kamakura Shogunate in the latter years of the twelfth century, Masatsune's talents—in both kickball and poetry—led to recognition by Retired Emperor Go-Toba, who selected him as one of the compilers of the *Shin kokinshū*.

Go-Toba was somewhat reticent in his praise for Masatsune; but he did credit him as "the kind of poet who pondered his compositions deeply, revising them again and again" (Brower 1972:37). Clearly Masatsune made good on his gifts, leaving a legacy that would last until the fifteenth century, when the Asukai family would become one of the last standard-bearers for the orthodox cause of the Nijō line.

Poems

SKKS 93 (SPRING) On travel, from a poem contest held at the Poetry Bureau

1
Over stones I tramped,
through mountain upon mountain—
and never looked back:
till behind me the blossoms
    became layers of white clouds.[1]

SKKS 483 (AUTUMN) On the idea of "Mallet Striking Robe"*

2
In fair Yoshino†
    autumn winds blow from the mountains
        late into the night;
and cold in the old capital—‡
the sound of mallet on robe.[2]

* Robes were fulled—beaten with a wooden mallet on a wooden block—in the autumn. In poetry, the image evoked by the sound of the mallet striking the block is the forlorn one of a wife cleaning the robes of a husband away from home.
† A mountainous area in central Yamato (modern Nara Perfecture).
‡ Yoshino village was the site of a capital in ancient times.

SKKS 1668 (MISCELLANEOUS) Presented as part of a fifty-poem sequence

3

Here all that prospers
  is the dew that glitters so
    in the rank grass—
reflecting the moon's decline
  around my abandoned home.[3]

SCSS 108 (SPRING) Topic unknown

4

The spring night ended
  with only the moon left
    in the sky at dawn—
while I spent my time idly,
  gazing out at faded flowers.[4]

SCSS 183 (SUMMER) On "Fireflies on an Inlet," composed for a fifty-poem sequence

5

Naniwa* women
  burn dead reeds† along the shore
    of a deep inlet;
and above, too, there is glowing—
  from fireflies in flight.

* *Ashi*. Common reeds found along ditches, inlets, swamps, etc.
† A coastal area in ancient Settsu (modern Ōsaka) known for its reeds.

6

Today autumn wanes:
with the Tatsuta's* waters
   tic-dyed red,† no doubt—
bringing a change of color
   even to its waves.[5]

* A mountainous area just southwest of the old capital at Nara that
was noted for its autumn leaves.
† An effect produced by crisscrossing bands of red leaves carried down
from the mountains by the river current.

SCSS 745 (LOVE) On the topic "Distant Love," composed in the Fourth
Month of the fifth year of the Kempō era [1217]

7

Which one of us
   can call the other cruel?
The one who won't come
   and the one who waits both grow old—
like the Takasago Pine.*

* A famous pine standing on the shore of ancient Harima (modern
Hyōgo Prefecture) in front of a Shinto shrine. In poetry, a symbol of
old age and longevity.

SCSS 1169 (MISCELLANEOUS) Presented as part of a hundred-poem sequence in the fourth year of the Kempō era [1216]

8
The great happiness
   that one was glad to wrap
in one's broad sleeves
   may in the end come to seem
a burden* too great to bear.[6]

* Perhaps referring to the happiness that comes with a promotion in court rank or office that is not followed by more advancements in coming years. Masatsune himself was promoted to the office of Consultant (*sangi*) only at age fifty, just a year before his death.

NOTES

1. An allusive variation on MYS 2422: "Between the two of us / are no mountains to be crossed / like stones to tramp over— / and yet how I long for you / when for days we do not meet!" (*Iwanefumu / kasanaru yama wa / aranedomo / awanu hi manemi / koishiwataru kamo.*)

2. An allusive variation on KKS 325, by Sakanoue no Korenori (tenth century) [Headnote: Composed at his lodgings when he went to the Nara capital]: "The white flakes of snow / in fair Yoshino's mountains / must be piling high, / for cold strikes ever sharper / at the ancient capital." (*Miyoshino no / yama no shirayuki / tsumorurashi / furusato samuku / narimasaru nari.*) McCullough 1985:79.

3. An allusive variation on KKS 200, anonymous [Headnote: Topic unknown]: "Waiting-insect cries / fall poignantly on the ear / at the old dwelling, / buried in remembrance ferns, / where I grow thin with longing." (*Kimi shinobu / kusa ni yatsururu / furusato wa / matsumushi no ne zo / kanashikarikeru.*) McCullough 1985:53.

4. An allusive variation on KKS 113, by Ono no Komachi (fl. ca. 850): "Alas! The beauty / of the flowers has faded / and come to nothing / while I have watched the rain / lost in melancholy thought." (*Hana no iro wa / utsurinikeri na / itazura ni / wa ga mi yo ni furu / nagame seshi ma ni.*) McCullough 1985:35.

5. An allusive variation on KKS 294, by Ariwara no Narihira

[Headnote: Composed when the Nijō Empress was still called the Mother of the Crown Prince. Topic set: A folding-screen picture of autumn leaves floating on the Tatsuta River]: "There was not the like / even in the fabled age / of the mighty gods: / this fine red pattern dyed / in Tatsuta's waters." (*Chihayaburu / kamiyo mo kikazu / tatsutagawa / karakurenai ni / mizu kukuru to wa.*) McCullough 1985:72.

6. An allusive variation on KKS 365, anonymous [Headnote: Topic unknown]: "In what might I wrap / the great happiness I feel? / Had I foreseen it, / I would have said, "Make wide sleeves / on this robe of Chinese silk." (*Ureshiki o / nani ni tsutsumamu / karakoromo / tamoto yutaka ni / tate o iwamashi o.*) McCullough 1985:88.

JAPANESE TEXTS

1 Iwane fumi / kasanaru yama o / wakesutete / hana mo ikue no / ato no shirakumo

2 Miyoshino no / yama no akikaze / sayo fukete / furusato samuku / koromo utsu nari

3 Kage yadosu / tsuyu nomi shigeku / narihatete / kusa ni yatsururu / furusato no tsuki

4 Haru no yo no / tsuki mo ariake ni / narinikeri / utsurou hana ni / nagame seshi ma ni

5 Naniwame ga / sugumo taku hi no / fukaki ni ni / ue ni moete mo / yuku hotaru kana

6 Aki wa kyō / kurenai kururu / tatsutagawa / yuku se no nami mo / iro kawaruran

7 Tsurenashi to / tare o ka iwamu / takasago no / matsu mo itou mo / toshi wa henikeri

8 Ureshisa mo / tsutsuminarenishi / sode ni mata / hate wa amari no / mi o zo uramuru

CONTESTANTS

Fujiwara no Tameie

Fujiwara no Tameuji

Kyōgoku Tamenori

Nun Abutsu

Reizei Tamesuke

Fujiwara no Tameie (1198–1275)

As a young man, Fujiwara no Tameie, born the heir of Teika, disappointed his father by spending more energy on *kemari* (an elegant form of kickball) than on poetry. It was only from about age twenty on that he began to take his family tradition more seriously. After his father's death in 1241, however, he came into his own, participating in most of the important poetic events at court, where he often served as contest judge and critic. Along with his high reputation came advancements in rank and office: in 1241 he was granted Senior Second rank, and by 1250 he was Minister of Popular Affairs and a Provisional Major Counselor, a position his father had never been able to attain.

Following family custom, Tameie became a compiler of two imperial anthologies, *Shoku gosenshū* (Later Collection Continued, 1251) and *Shoku kokinshū* (Collection of Ancient and Modern Times Continued, 1265). The former work, which he compiled alone, became one of the most highly revered anthologies among Nijō poets, who saw it as a nearly perfect expression of their philosophy.[1] Had he been given his way, the *Shoku kokinshū* would also have been a product of his own individual effort. But other powerful poets, most notably Rokujō Tomoie (1182–1258) and his son Yukiie (1223–1275), used their influence with the Kamakura shogunate to thwart his ambitions. In the end, Tameie had to share credit for the collection with Yukiie and several others, and throughout the rest of his life his position at court was occasionally challenged by rivals in other poetic houses.

In 1256 Tameie was stricken with a serious illness that moved him to take the tonsure, although he lived for another twenty years, most of which he spent at a family estate in Saga. It was during this period that he developed a special attachment to An-kamon'in no Shijō, a woman known to history as the Nun Abutsu (d. 1283). One result of this late romance was a son, Tamesuke (1263–1328). Tameie doted on the little boy, and as a sign of his affection willed to him not only the rights to revenues from several important estates but also treasured poetic documents handed down from Shunzei and Teika. It was the contest over possession of those revenues and documents that began the long conflict between the Nijō and Reizei houses.[2]

In his one major critical work, *Yakumo kuden* (Teachings on the Art of the Eightfold Clouds; alternative title, *Eiga no ittei*, The Foremost Style of Poetic Composition), Tameie praises poems in the plain manner of what was to become the Nijō style.[3] In later ages he was held up as a model by those who hesitated to put forth Teika—a more difficult poet by any standards—in the same way.[4]

NOTES

1. *Kinrai fūtei, NKT* 5:143.
2. See my introduction and Brower 1981:447–451 for details.
3. See *Yakumo kuden, NKT* 3:388–401. For a full translation of the work, see Brower 1987.
4. See Tonna's *Seiashō, NKT* 5:93.

Poems

SCSS 383 (WINTER) From among his Winter poems

> 1
> After winter comes,
> there may be a rare break
>   in the rain clouds,
> but even then no day goes by
>   without showers of falling leaves.

SHOKUGSS 124 (SPRING) On "Blossoms in the Garden," from a fifty-poem sequence composed at the home of the Reverend Prince Dōjō

> 2
> The footprints are gone
>   from my unvisited garden—
> the color of the moss
>   now all but forgotten
>   beneath fallen blossoms.[1]

SHOKUGSS 536 (SHINTO) On "The Moon at a Famous Place," from a
poetry contest at the home of the Lay Priest—Former Regent

3
Isuzu River:*
like a mirror left behind
    from the Age of the Gods,†
it shows the unclouded image
    of the moon on an autumn night.[2]

* A river in Ise (modern Mie Prefecture), running by Ise Shrine.
† The mythical age during which the Japanese Islands were created.

SHOKUGSS 562 (SHINTO) Jotted down and left on a visit to the Miwa
Shrine*

4
Dangling sacred cords,†
the cedars around the shrine
    are now full of years.
And this itself is a sign
    left from the Age of the Gods.

* The oldest of all native shrines, located in modern Nara Prefecture.
† *Mishime*. Straw ropes used to cordon off sacred objects or areas within
the shrine precincts.

5

In the river rapids
    the waves are washing over
        a bankside boulder;
and spilling down on it—
    kerria in full bloom.

* *Yamabuki*. A yellow wildflower with five-petaled blossoms resembling a rose in shape.

SHOKUKKS 219 (SUMMER) On "Hearing a Cuckoo While Awake in the Night," from a fifty-poem sequence

6

A cuckoo* calls out—
but its voice does not signal
    that day has begun.
Much of the night is left
    to an old man's wakefulness.[3]

* *Hototogisu*. A small bird of the cuckoo family whose plaintive song was highly admired by poets.

From among the poems of a ten-poem sequence written on the thirteenth day of the Ninth Month, at Akashi Bay*

7

To Akashi's strand
   I came in hope of finding
      remnants of the past—
and tonight again the full moon
     shines in the tears on my sleeves.[4]

* An area on the coast of the Inland Sea just west of modern Kōbe.

Written on one of the topics of *The Six Volumes of Poetry*

8

What am I to think?
Like the receding tide
   at Narumi Bay,†
so swiftly does the one I love
    pull away from me.

* *Kokin waka rokujō*. A large collection of poems from *Man'yōshū*, *Kokinshū*, and *Gosenshū*, arranged by thematic and lexical categories. Used as a primer and handbook by poets.
† A bay on the coast of Owari, near present Nagoya.

9

I had lost myself
  reminiscing on the past—
and then I heard
  a cuckoo* raising its voice
    far off in the distant clouds.[5]

* *Hototogisu.* This small bird's call was believed to evoke memories of
the past.

SHOKUSIS 276 (AUTUMN) On "Haze," presented as part of a hundred-
poem sequence in the first year of the Kōchō era [1261]

10

In dawn's early glow
  the peak of Storm Mountain*
    comes into the clear—
while coming down to its base
  is the autumn river mist.[6]

* Arashiyama. A mountain just west of the capital, along the Ōi River.

SHOKUSIS 568 (MISCELLANEOUS-AUTUMN) On "Reeds," presented as part of a hundred-poem sequence in the first year of the Kōchō era [1261]

11
Always in the past
   I was startled from my sleep
      by the rustling reeds*—
now I lie awake in the night
      waiting for the wind.

* *Ogi.* A large flowering grass resembling *susuki* (miscanthus) in shape and features.

SHOKUSIS 897 (LOVE) On "Pining for Love," from a ten-poem sequence written at the home of the Yamashina Lay Priest–Former Minister of the Left

12
Yes, but all the same,*
though all my nights of turmoil
   have come to nothing,
I will believe to the end—
   even in his lies.

* An elliptical phrase meaning, "He cannot be trusted—I know; but all the same I will go on . . ."

13
Even the dead leaves
of the flowers on the altar shelf*
are wet through now—
so thick is the morning dew
at the mountain-top temple.

* A shelf just outside the altar upon which flowers and water were placed for preparation before being presented as offerings.

NOTES

1. An allusive variation on KKS 287, anonymous [Headnote: Topic unknown]: "Now autumn has come. / Fallen colored foliage / carpets the garden, / and along the buried path / no visitor makes his way." (*Aki wa kinu / momiji wa yado ni / furishikinu / michi fumiwakete / tou hito wa nashi.*) McCullough 1985:71.

2. An allusive variation on SKKS 1880, by Archbishop Jien, in which he praises the moon as shining with the "softened light" of the Japanese Sun Goddess Amaterasu, who was a transformation of the bodhisattva Vairocana, according to Buddhist doctrine. [Headnote: Written as a Shinto poem]: "Surely its rays / are left over from the softer light / of the Sun Goddess—this moon on an autumn night / shining on Izumi River." (*Yamaraguru / hikari ni amaru / kage nare ya / isuzugawara no / aki no yo no tsuki.*)

3. An allusive variation on KKS 156, by Ki no Tsurayuki (ca. 868–946) [Headnote: A poem from the Empress' Contest during the reign of the Kanpyō Emperor]: "On a summer night, / no sooner have I lain down / than the first faint light / of dawn appears—heralded / by a cuckoo's single song." (*Natsu no yo no / fusu ka to sureba / hototogisu / naku hitokoe ni / akuru shinonome.*) McCullough 1985:44.

4. A reference to the "Akashi" chapter of *The Tale of Genji*. See Seidensticker 1976, 1:247–270.

5. An echo of SZS 191, by Master of Discipline Kyōsen (precise dates unknown) [Headnote: Written upon hearing a cuckoo sing at Kaguraoka, when he was on his way to the Bodaizu Cloister to hear the

Eight Expositions at the time of Retired Emperor Go-Ichijō]: "While I was alone / thinking fondly of the past, / I crossed the peak— / and was met there by the voice / of a mountain cuckoo." (*Inishie o / koitsutsu hitori / koekureba / nakiau yama no / hototogisu kana.*)

6. An allusion to SG 1487, by Teika. See poem 44 by Fujiwara no Teika in this anthology.

JAPANESE TEXTS

1 Fuyu kite wa / shigururu kumo no / taema dani / yo mo no konoha no / furanu hi zo naki

2 Ato taete / towarenu niwa no / koke no iro mo / wasuru bakari ni / niwa zo furishiku

3 Isuzugawa / kamiyo no kagami / kaketomete / ima mo kumoranu / aki no yo no tsuki

4 Mishime hiku / miwa no sugimura / furinikeri / kore ya kamiyo no / shirushi naruramu

5 Hayasegawa / nami no kagehosu / iwakishi ni / koborete sakeru / yamabuki no hana

6 Hototogisu / naku hitokoe mo / akeyarazu / nao yo o nokosu / oi no nezame ni

7 Akashigata / mukashi no ato o / tazunekite / koyoi mo tsuki ni / sode nurashitsuru

8 Iza shirazu / narumi no ura ni / hiku shio no / hayaku zo hito wa / tōzakarinishi

9 Inishie o / omoiizureba / hototogisu / kumoi haruka ni / ne koso nakarure

10 Asaborake / arashi no yama wa / mine harete / fumoto o kudaru / aki no kawagiri

11 Inishie wa / odorokasareshi / ori no ha ni / fukikuru kaze o / nezame ni zo matsu

12 Saritomo to / omou kai naki / yoiyoi no / itsuwari o dani / tanomihatebaya

13 Akadana no / hana no kareba mo / uchishimeri / asatsuyu fukashi / mine no yamadera

Fujiwara no Tameuji (1222–1286)

The road to literary success for Fujiwara no Tameuji was similar to the one followed by his father and grandfather. Born the heir of Tameie —and grandson of Teika—he was instructed by both men from an early age, and in time gained the prominence that was expected of him as inheritor of the Mikohidari house. The presence of two brothers—Tamenori (1227–1279), founder of the Kyōgoku line, and Tamesuke, founder of the Reizei line— who constituted a constant challenge to his authority made his life difficult at times; and his relations with Tameie, toward whom he appears to have been less than properly filial in attitude and demeanor, were not close after the latter's retirement to Saga. For most of his life, however, his status as heir of the main house gave him ascendance over his rivals.

Like his father, Tameuji was granted the office of Provisional Major Counselor, Senior Second rank. He was chief compiler of the *Shoku shūishū* (Collection of Gleanings Continued, 1278) and also a contest judge and scholar with powerful patrons among the higher aristocratic families.

It was a sign of the times that Tameuji also had close contacts among the warrior families of the eastern seaboard, mostly through his maternal grandfather, Utsunomiya Yoritsuna (1179–1259), whose estates in Shimotsuke the poet visited at least twice—once in his teens and again toward the end of his life—for extended periods. He died in Kamakura.

Tameuji's decision to include many poems by his maternal grandfather and other eastern warriors in the *Shoku shūishū* angered some of his aristocratic friends, who accused him of nepotism, if not bad taste. And even his most famous poem (*Shoku gosenshū* 41, translated below) is reported to have gained its current form only with Tameie's revision (*Seiāshō, NKT* 5:95). Although his importance in literary politics has guaranteed Tameuji mention in the annals of medieval poetic history, not even his own Nijō heirs afforded him the highest praise as an artist.

Poems

SHOKUGSS 41 (SPRING) On "A Spring View of an Inlet," written in the second year of the Kenchō era [1250] for a contest involving Chinese and Japanese poems

> 1
> If anyone asks,
> I should say I haven't seen it*—
> Tamazu Isle,†
> where haze spreads over the inlet
>   in the dim light of a spring dawn.[1]

* The implication being that the scene would be too beautiful to describe in words.
† A small island in Wakanoura Bay, Kii (modern Wakayama Prefecture).

SHOKUGSS 830 (LOVE) On the idea of "Love, the Morning After"

> 2
> Did it not signal
>   that the time to leave has come,
> I would not see it
>   as only a cause of sadness—
> that moon shining at dawn.[2]

SHOKUSIS 129 (SPRING) On "Spring Moon," written as part of a hundred-poem sequence at the imperial palace in the third year of the Kōchō era [1263]

3

On a spring night,
from the gaps in the haze
    it shows a faint glimpse
of a distant mountain crest—
the light of the rising moon.

SHOKUSIS 330 (AUTUMN) On "Autumn Cold in a Paddy Hut," from a ten-poem sequence composed at the home of the Yamashina Lay Priest–Former Minisiter of the Left

4

The dew and the frost
    have brought color to the leaves*
        of the late rice plants;
how cold is my little hut
    amidst autumn's mountain winds![3]

* Dew, showers, and frost were deemed responsible for leaves changing color in autumn.

Presented as one of the poems of a hundred-poem sequence presented in the first year of the Kōchō era [1261]

5

"Not a leaf shall stay—
not even as a memento
   of autumn's glory"—
so it seems to be saying,
this withering winter wind![4]

On "Celebration in the Moonlight," presented as part of a ten-poem sequence at the imperial palace on the night of the thirteenth day of the Ninth Month of the third year of the Kōchō Era [1263]

6

Since the moon resides
   high up in those same clouds*
      where dwells our Lord,
it has shone through the ages—
an unchanging light.

* *Kumoi.* Literally, "the clouds"; here, used as an epithet for the imperial court.

SGSS 1 (SPRING) Composed on a day when spring arrived during the old year*

7

The Sao Princess†
　　has donned her new robe of haze
　　　　while it's still winter:
　to a sky looking like snow
　　　the springtime has come.

* In years when an intercalary month was added into the calendar to make up for the extra days in the lunar years, the equinox—marking the beginning of spring—often came before the end of the old year.
† The Goddess of Spring, who made her abode on Sao Mountain to the east of the old capital at Nara, the direction of spring in Chinese thought.

SGSS 745 (SHINTO) Topic unknown

8

At Sasanami*
　　the pines are just as they were
　　　　in the Age of the Gods—
　and also as in olden times
　　is the wind along the bay.[5]

* Located on the southern tip of Lake Biwa, site of an ancient capital (modern Shiga Prefecture).

NOTES

1. An allusive variation on MYS 1215, anonymous: "At Tamazu Isle / look well at what you see! / —for what will you say / if back in Nara of the rich earth / someone should ask it of you?" (*Tamazushima / yoku mite imase / aoniyoshi / nara naru hito no / machitowaba ika ni.*)

2. An allusive variation on KKS 625, by Mibu no Tadamine [Headnote: Topic unknown]: "The hours before dawn / seem saddest of all to me / since that leave-taking / when I saw in the heavens / the pale moon's indifferent face." (*Ariake no / tsurenaku mieshi / wakare yori / akatsuki bakari / uki mono wa nashi.*) McCullough 1985:140.

3. An allusion to MYS 2174, attributed to Emperor Tenchi: "For a short stay / I make myself a paddy-hut / in the autumn fields: / and how cold are my sleeves / covered so with dew!" (*Akita karu / kariho o tsukuri / waga oreba / koromode samuku / tsuyu zo okinikeru.*) See also GSS 302.

4. An allusive variation on SZS 388, by Minamoto no Toshiyori (1055–1129) [Headnote: Written on the topic "Early Winter," for a hundred-poem sequence presented during the time of Retired Emperor Horikawa]: "How would I have seen / this last memento / of autumn's glory? / —if storm winds had not blown / through the leaves this morning!" (*Ikabakari / aki no nagori o / nagamemashi / kesa wa konoha ni / arashi fukazu wa.*) The "memento" here is the moon, which becomes fully visible after all the leaves have been blown from the trees.

5. An echo of the envoy to a famous *chōka* (MYS 30) entitled "On Passing the Ruined Capital at Ōmi," by Kakinomoto Hitomaro: "At Sasanami, / Cape Karasaki ni Shiga / is as it ever was— / yet it waits to no avail / for the courtiers in their boats." (*Sasanami no / shiga no karasaki / sakiku wa aredo / ōmiyahito no / fune machikanetsu.*)

JAPANESE TEXTS

1 Hito towaba / mizu to ya iwamu / tamazushima / kasumu irie no / haru no akebono

2 Kinuginu no / wakare shi naku wa / uki mono to / iwade zo mimashi / ariake no tsuki

3 Haru no yo no / kasumi no ma yori / yama no ha o / honoka ni misete / izuru tsukikage

4 Tsuyu shimo no / okute no inabe / irozukite / kariio samuki / aki no yamakaze

5 Momijiba no / aki no nagori no / katami dani / ware to nokosanu /
kogarashi no kaze
6 Kimi ga sumu / onaji kumoi no / tsuki nareba / sora ni kawaranu /
yorozuyo no kage
7 Saohime no / kasumi no koromo / fuyu kakete / yukige no sora ni /
haru wa kinikeri
8 Sasanami ya / kamiyo no matsu no / sono mama ni / mukashi nagara
no / urakaze zo fuku

Kyōgoku Tamenori (1227–1279)

Like his elder brother Tameuji, Tamenori was born to Tameie's first wife, a daughter of Utsunomiya Yoritsuna. Despite the close blood relationship between the brothers, however, they did not get along. In time, Tamenori broke away from the main house and formed his own separate branch of the family—called the Kyōgoku, after the location of his home in Kyōto. So great was the animosity between the two men that Tamenori was often excluded from participation in Nijō poetry contests and gatherings.

Tamenori seems to have had little contact with his mother's family, who understandably supported the claims of the senior line. Thus he seems to have had few contacts in Kamakura. In the capital, on the other hand, he had a number of powerful patrons to rely upon, most especially the Saionji family, for whom he served as a steward. With such support, he became an important figure in poetic circles, although never so central a one as Tameuji himself. As the heir to a junior line of the Mikohidari house, he was only able to rise as high as Junior Second rank.

Tamenori's conflicts with Tameuji came to a climax during the time the latter was compiling the *Shoku shūishū*, from 1276 to 1278. Complaining that the Kyōgoku and Reizei families were not being fairly represented in the anthology, Tamenori petitioned the Poetry Bureau for revisions, but to no avail. He died just a year later, with his requests still unanswered.

It says something about his estimation of his own talent that Tamenori asked the Poetry Bureau to delete some of his own poems from the *Shoku shūishū* in return for augmenting the representation of his children—Tameko (d. 1316) and Tamekane (1254–1332). His descriptive nature poems in some ways seem to presage the full Kyōgoku style, but to this day his place in poetic history has been dependent less on his own modest gifts than on the reputation of his children.

Poems

From among his Summer poems

1

Over heavy dew
on the weeds* in my garden,
the wind passes
leaving coolness in its wake
in the stormy evening sky.

* *Asaji.* Cogon grass—a short reed-like plant that grows in clumps on moorlands and meadows. In poetry, it carries a melancholy connotation and is generally shown thriving around run-down or abandoned homes.

SHOKUSIS 1088 (LOVE) From among his Love poems

2

Enough—so be it!
I will simply leave and say
the fault was all mine—
but with your indifference
as a memento of our love.

3

In the dusky light,
the gate paddies* at Fushimi†
    are gently swaying;
and traversing those rice-ear waves,
a boat on Uji River.‡[1]

* *Kadota*. Rice paddies near the front gate of a residence.
† A rural area just south of Kyōto, famous for its pastoral beauty.
‡ A river running through the Uji area that here—in an elegant "confusion of the senses" reminiscent of earlier ages of Japanese poetry—cannot be seen because of the high rice plants, making it appear that a passing boat is being poled along through the waves of their own swaying plumes.

GYS 810 (AUTUMN) On "Insect Voices Growing Weak in the Garden"

4

As autumn wears on,
there are crickets in the weeds*
    in my garden.
How cold the night must be
    for their voices to sound so weak![2]

* *Asaji*.

5
Above in the clear
   of the arching high night sky—
not a shadow of a cloud;
but here in shade of the trees—
a shower of winter moonlight.

NOTES

1. An allusive variation on KYS 173, by Minamoto no Tsunenobu (1016–1097) [Headnote: Written on "Autumn at a House in the Paddies"]: "As night settles in, / there is a sound in the plumes / of the gate paddies: / past a reed-thatched shack / blows the autumn wind" (*Yūsareba / kadota no inaba / otozurete / ashi no maroya / ukikaze zo fuku.*)

2. An allusive variation on SKKS 535, by Sone no Yoshitada (fl. ca. 980–1000) [Headnote: Topic unknown]: "No one ever comes; / and the leaves are all gone now, / scattered on the wind. / Night after night, the voices / of the insects sound more weak." (*Hito wa kozu / kaze ni konoha wa / chirihatete / yona yona mushi wa / koe yowaru nari.*)

JAPANESE TEXTS

1 Tsuyu fukaki / niwa no asaji ni / kaze sugite / nagori suzushiki / yūdachi no sora

2 Yoshi saraba / waga mi no toga ni / iinasan / tsurasa o hito no / omoide ni shite

3 Kurekakaru / fushimi no kadota / uchinabiki / honami o wataru / uji no kawa fune

4 Aki fukuru / asaji ga niwa no / kirigirisu / yo ya samukarashi / koe yowariyuku

5 Suminoboru / sora ni wa kumoru / kage mo nashi / kokage shigururu / fuyu no yo no tsuki

Nun Abutsu (d. ca. 1283)

As is the case with so many women of her time, the precise background of the court lady now known as the Nun Abutsu is obscure. Documents indicate that she was raised by one Taira no Norishige, a low-ranking courtier of the provincial governor class. We also know that she served in her teens as a lady-in-waiting to Ex-Empress (an honorary title) Ankamon'in, whence she herself received the lay name Ankamon'in no Shijō. After being rejected by a lover, she retired from society for a time. Thereafter she seems to have accompanied Norishige to the provinces for a brief period.

Her importance in literary history began sometime around 1253, when she became a wife to Fujiwara no Tameie, son of Teika and chief heir of the Mikohidari house. For the next twenty-two years, until Tameie's death in 1275, she was in most ways his closest confidante, and one of the sons she bore him in his last years—Tamesuke—was one of the great joys of his life. An astute and careful protector, Ankamon'in no Shijō convinced Tameie to leave her son estate rights and poetic documents that would assure him a place in the scheme of things after Tameie's own death, thus creating a situation that would lead to major conflicts with Tameuji, heir of the Mikohidari house.

After Tameie's death, Ankamon'in no Shijō took holy orders as the Nun Abutsu, albeit remaining very much involved in the world all the same. When Tameuji's challenge of Tameie's will met with success among his imperial patrons in Kyōto, she personally made the long trip to Kamakura to seek redress from the military government. Her diary of that journey, entitled *Izayoi nikki* (Diary of the Waning Moon), is considered a minor court classic.[1] Four of the poems quoted below are taken from its pages.

Abutsu died, probably in Kamakura, before ever hearing the verdict in her son's case, which turned out to be a positive one, handed down in 1289.[2] But she left her son a strong legacy all the same. Not a great poet, she is nonetheless an important figure in poetic history, rightly recognized as the founder of the Reizei house. In her critical work, entitled *Yoru no tsuru* (Night Crane), she emphasized the need for refinement of feeling and depiction of nature as it is (*ari no mama*), two ideas that were to guide her descendants for generations to come.[3]

NOTES

1. For a translation of this work, see Reischauer and Yamagiwa 1951.
2. A Kyōto court reversed this decision in 1291, forcing Tamesuke to file a countersuit that returned to him his rights only after he was fifty years old. See Brower 1981: 450.
3. See NKT 3:407.

Poems

GYS 1134 (TRAVEL) When she was on her way to the East Country,* she passed through a place called Noji.† It was getting dark, and on top of that rain started to fall.

> 1
> A shower comes up,
> drenching my sleeves with its rain
>   as I long for home;
> and still far from journey's end
>   is Noji's Bamboo Moor.

* Azuma. A term referring in a general way to the provinces east of Kyōto; here, more specifically, to the area around Kamakura, seat of the shogunal government at the time.
† Just to the east of the capital, in Ōmi (modern Shiga Prefecture).

GYS 1135 (TRAVEL) While fording Yasu River* on the way to the East Country, a mist obscured the crossing so much that they could only hear the sounds of people up ahead. She wrote her thoughts down in this poem:

> 2
> The travelers
>   are all up and on their way
>   early this morning—
> urging their ponies ahead
>   through the mist on Yasu River.

* Yasukawa. A river in Ōmi (on the border between modern Shiga and Mie Prefectures), just east of Kyōto.

GYS 1216 (TRAVEL) When she was on her way to the East Country, she noticed a large group of cormorants on the beach, a most captivating sight:

> 3
> Against the white beach—
> the ink-black colors
>   of the island birds:
> were I skillful with my brush,
> I would paint them in a picture.

4

In the former world*
  who bound me to such a fate?
—to the anguish
  of living on with no one
    to untie my undersash.†

* *Saki no yo*. In Buddhist terms, a previous existence—to which poets often appeal to make sense of this one.
† To untie one's undersash (*shitahimo*) was a metaphor for giving one's body to a man. The belief was that when a woman was loved by a man, her sash would come undone of itself.

GYS 1455, 1456 (LOVE) After being drenched by showers at dawn when returning home from her house, Tameie sent this poem later that morning:

5

On my way back home
  in the darkness before dawn,
the gathering clouds
  began to drop their showers—
on my own sleeves, first of all.

Her reply:

6

As you went away
  in the darkness before dawn,
leaving me behind,
  the tears I sent after you
    could well have caused that shower.

From *Diary of the Waning Moon* [Written while she was on her way to the East Country to plead the case of her children before the Shōgun]*

7

If not so my children
    may give service to my Lord
        in coming generations,
    then why would I make this trip
        past Fujikawa Barrier?†[1]

* This bracketed headnote is my summary of the situation in which the poem was written. See my introduction to Nun Abutsu for details.
† Seki no Fujikawa. A stream running near the famous Fuwa Barrier in Mino (modern Gifu Prefecture).

NOTES

1. An allusion to KKS 1084, a "Mino song sung at the Gangyō Thanksgiving" [Headnote: A song in a modulated key?]: "We shall serve our lord / for countless generations, / ceaselessly as flows / the barrier's Fuji River / in the Province of Mino." (*Mino no kuni / seki no fujikawa / taezu shite / kimi ni tsukaemu / yorozuyo made ni /*.) McCullough 1985:242.

JAPANESE TEXTS

1 Uchishigure / furusato omou / sode nurete / yukusaki tōki / noji no shinohara
2 Tabibito mo / mina morotomo ni / asatachite / koma uchiwatasu / yasu no kawakiri
3 Shirahama ni / sumi no iro naru / shimatsudori / fude mo oyobaba / e ni kakitemashi
4 Saki no yo ni / tare musebiken / shitashimo no / tokenu tsurasa o / mi no chigiri to wa

5 Kaerusa no / shinonome kuraki / murakumo mo / waga sode yori ya / shiguresometsuru

6 Kinuginu no / shinonome kuraki / wakareji ni / soeshi namida wa / sazo shigureken

7 Waga kodomo / kimi ni tsukaen / tame narade / wataramashi ya wa / seki no fujikawa

Reizei Tamesuke (1263–1328)

A full forty years the junior of his elder brother Tameuji, Tamesuke, literal founder of the Reizei line, began life at a disadvantage. Though cared for by his father, Tameie, who began instructing him at the age of three, he could not be expected to compete against the entrenched power of the Nijō house. It was his vulnerable situation after Tameie's death in 1275 that motivated his mother's journey to Kamakura to plead his interests before the shōgun several years later.

Although in the long term Tamesuke's petitions for restoration of at least some estate rights were successful, he was forced to yield to the main house often in his younger years, turning over to them not only revenues but also some poetic documents (among them a number of elegantly disguised forgeries). Unable to make a name for himself in the Nijō-dominated capital, he traveled to Kamakura, where over the years he had become a leading poetic figure among the families of the military government. In particular, he was close to the Imperial Prince Hisaakira, who served as shōgun from 1289 to 1308.

When he requested to be included among the compilers of an imperial anthology in 1294, Tamesuke was turned down with little explanation. And although he spent some time back in Kyōto in the early years of the fourteenth century, financial difficulties again sent him back to the East Country in 1308. There he was close to not only the shōgun but also the Hōjō family, whom he served as a tutor in uta composition and also as an early *rengashi,* or master of linked verse. Throughout his life he maintained cordial relations with the Kyōgoku family, despite differences in political affiliation; but, to the end, the intransigence of the Nijō house left him feeling bitter and abused.

Stylistically, Tamesuke favored the impressionistic realism of his Kyōgoku allies in his younger years, turning back to the more bland ways of the Nijō family in his old age. But, above all, his poems are evidence of the new influence of the Kamakura families on court poetry. He himself compiled two anthologies of his own poems and those of his friends in the military houses— *Shūi fūtei wakashō* (Gleanings of Elegant Styles, 1302–1308) and *Ryūfū wakashō* (Collection of Willows and Wind, 1310); and his own work shows the influence of provincial culture in both thematics and diction. His heirs continued the tradition of service to the great families of the east, contributing a fresh if sometimes overly prosaic quality to the poetry of the next two centuries.

Poems

GYS 2206 (MISCELLANEOUS) On "Mountain Home" from *The Hundred-Poem Sequences of the Kagen Era* [1303]*

1

The sun must be setting
   on the path into the hills
      near my little hut:
down to my eaves comes the sound
   of woodgatherer's voices.

* Referring to a number of such sequences commissioned from Tamesuke and others by Retired Emperor Go-Uda (1267–1324) in preparation for the compilation of the *Shin gosenshū*.

GYS 2530 (MISCELLANEOUS) From among his Miscellaneous poems

2

Born into the world
   when my mother's breasts were heavy*
      with the weight of old age,
I regret not being with her
   for the many years to come.

* *Tarachine no.* A fixed epithet for "mother," which here seems also to be used for its literal meaning of "drooping breasts."

From among his Winter poems

3
The showers go on
    until a break in the clouds
        shows the winter sun—
so weak that its light fades
    before the clouds can close again.

From among his Miscellaneous poems

4
In the valley shades,
it hides itself away
    back among the trees,
calling out for rain—
the voice of a mountain dove.[1]

RW (AUTUMN)

5
In this mountain village
    not even a storm passing by
        disturbed my dreams;
but what does wake me from sleep
    is the call of a stag.[2]

RW (AUTUMN) One day a group of people gathered together to talk. In the evening, with the moon hidden by clouds, everyone went to bed— except the poet, who stayed up alone until the sky cleared, and wrote this poem.

6

I wish I could tell
    those who went off to their beds
because of the clouds
    that now, late into the night,
the moon is shining clear.

FYS 15 (SPRING) On the topic "Spring Snow," presented as part of a hundred-poem sequence in the first year of the Kagen era [1303]

7

The mountain winds
    blow them about in the sky
and they disappear
    before reaching my garden—
light flakes of spring snow.

8

How can it be
that the showers have fallen
on this tree alone?
Before the hills have turned,
red leaves in my garden.*

* Dew, showers, and frost were deemed responsible for leaves changing color in autumn.

NOTES

1. An echo of SKKS 1676, by Monk Saigyō [Headnote: Topic unknown]: "From a tree standing / near paddies gone to seed / I hear a dove / calling out for a friend— / a forlorn sound at nightfall." (*Furuhata no / soba no tatsu ki ni / iru hato no / tomo yobu koe no / sugoki yūgure.*)

2. A possible allusion to SKKS 356, by Go-Kyōgoku Yoshitsune (1169–1206) [Headnote: From among poems presented as a hundred-poem sequence]: "With the wind blowing / a storm in the leaves of the reeds, / autumn seemed harsh enough— / and then, as if waiting his moment, / a stag called out in the night." (*Ogi no ha ni / fukeba arashi no / aki naru o / machikeru yowa no / saoshika no koe.*)

JAPANESE TEXTS

1 Io chikaki / tsumagi no michi ya / kurenuran / nokiba ni kudaru / yamabito no koe

2 Tarachine no / oi no yowari ni / mumareaite / hisashiku sowanu / mi o zo uramuru

3 Shigureyuku / kumoma ni yowaki / fuyu no hi no / kageroiaezu / kururu sora kana

4 Tanikage ya / kobukaki kata ni / kakuroete / ame o moyōsu / yamabato no koe

5 Arashi ni mo / yume wa kayoishi / yamazato no / nezame to naru
   wa / saoshika no koe
6 Fukete kaku / harekeru tsuki o / kumoru tote / neya ni iritsuru / hito
   ni tsugeba ya
7 Yamakaze no / fukimaku sora ni / katsu kiete / niwa made furanu /
   haru no awayuki
8 Ika ni shite / kono hitomoto no / shigureken / yama ni sakidatsu /
   niwa no momijiba

COMRADES

Kyōgoku Tamekane

Kyōgoku Tameko

Jūsammi Chikako

Emperor Fushimi

Empress Eifuku

Kyōgoku Tamekane (1254–1332)

By all accounts one of the most original of medieval poets, Kyōgoku Tamekane, son of Tamenori, was also one of the age's most forceful personalities, a man whose precocious talent had a profound impact on an entire generation.

Such talent of course needed a protector, whom the young man found in Crown Prince Hirohito of the Jimyō-In line. Entering the service of the prince in 1280 through the offices of Saionji Sanekane (1249–1332), another patron, Tamekane rapidly established himself as poetic tutor to a lively salon of courtiers and ladies. When the prince ascended the throne as Emperor Fushimi in 1287, Tamekane rose in prominence with him. By 1291 he held the title of Provisional Midddle Counselor; two years later he was among those commissioned to compile a new imperial anthology.

Thus his career began with great promise. In the event, however, political resistance from the Nijō house kept the anthology from coming into being, and within several years, Tamekane, a victim of slander, found himself stripped of offices and sent into exile to the remote isle of Sado. Even after he returned to the capital in 1303 it was to a Daikakuji administration unresponsive to his ambitions. His friends around the now Retired Emperor Fushimi were reduced to a minority party.

This political alienation, however, had the predictable effect of turning the energies of Tamekane and his patrons toward poetry. Thus it was at this time, during the early years of the fourteenth century, that the Kyōgoku style was born.[1] By the time

Emperor Hanazono (1297–1348), one of Fushimi's sons, ascended the throne in 1308, the Jimyō-In line was prepared to make a statement, which, as one might expect, took the form of an imperial anthology—*Gyokuyōshū* (Collection of Jeweled Leaves, 1313). Over Nijō protests, Tamekane was made sole compiler of the work, which is today almost universally recognized as the finest of all imperial anthologies after the *Shin kokinshū*.

Thus the Kyōgoku heir was vindicated. But before long he suffered another political defeat, this time after offending his old patron Saionji Sanekane, who had him once again sent into exile, to Tosa. This time there was no reprieve: although allowed to return as far as Kawachi, Tamekane died outside the capital, cut off from the poetic society that had been his life.

Tamekane's one extant poetic treatise was written in his younger years and does not fully present his mature style.[2] In its emphasis on honesty and directness of expression, however, it is representative of his philosophy. His impressionistic nature poems, with their emphasis on "objective" apprehension of slight movements in the landscape and the subtle play of light and shadow, are some of the finest of the court tradition.

NOTES

1. Iwasa 1976:24.
2. For a translation of the work, see Huey and Matisoff 1985. Huey 1987 presents a poem contest involving Tamekane and others.

Poems

Nomori no kagami 5, in SKKT 5

1
When one looks at it
   closely, ever so closely,
one will discover—
that a reed* is nothing more
   than a large miscanthus.†

* *Ogi.* A large flowering grass resembling *susuki* (miscanthus) in shape and features
† *Susuki.* A large plant resembling pampas grass that flowers each autumn in hills and fields.

From *Ei risshun hyakushu waka*[1]

2
From today forward
   we know that spring has begun;
and yet all the same—
not a thing has changed
   from what it was yesterday.

GYS 9 (SPRING) Written on "A Spring View from Back in the Hills"

> 3
> Even the bird calls
>   seem serene as the mountrain
>   opens to morning;
> and the color of the haze
>   has the look of spring.

GYS 83 (SPRING) On "Spring Rain," composed when he held a poem contest at his home

> 4
> On an evening
>   aglow with the crimson
>   of plum flowers,
> the willow boughs sway softly;
> and the spring rain falls.[2]

GYS 174 (SPRING) From among his Spring poems

> 5
> My mind is made up:
> of the four times of the year,
> flowery spring is best—
> and within the spring itself,
> I like the sky at dawn.[3]

GYS 292 (SPRING) Written on the night of the last day of the Third Month

6

Round and round time turns,
and so it may be that once more
    I shall meet spring.
But this day, this night,
these will never come again.

GYS 419 (SUMMER) From among his Summer poems

7

Sifting through branches,
the rays of the morning sun
    are still very few—
and how deep is the coolness
    back among the bamboos!

GYS 832 (AUTUMN) From a thirty-poem sequence on "Late Autumn"

8

In my heart I'll store
    the color of the grasses and trees*
        I gaze on now—
so that there at least
    their image will stay with me.

* *Kusaki.* Referring here to the leaves and grasses, the memory of whose bright colors the poet wants to store away against the bleakness of winter.

GYS 1010 (WINTER) From among his Winter poems

> 9
> In the snow piled up
>   on the roof above my head,
> it makes not a sound—
> but the slanting hail
>   does tap at my window.

GYS 1022 (WINTER) A poem written on the topic "Winter Trees," at a time when courtiers were "searching for topics"*

> 10
> Over empty limbs
>   where not a leaf still clings,
> the old year wanes;
> but soon spring will be here,
> blessing us with its new buds.

* *Dai o suguru.* An informal poem contest in which poets gathered to compose poems extemporaneously on topics written out, placed on a dais, and then chosen at random.

11
He passes the inn
    where he was to spend the night—
drawn on by the moon.
Already on tomorrow's path
    is the midnight traveler.[4]

12
With him bound by fear,
and I too much reserved
    to ask him to come,
this night we should be sharing
    simply wastes itself away.[5]

13
How many times
    have we met only to fear
        it was the last time?
Now the sadness we felt then
    no one else can know.

GYS 1706 (LOVE) On the topic "Bitterness Over Lost Love," from a thirty-poem sequence

14
Those bitter feelings
   I gave vent to in my words
      have faded away—
turned now into grief
   locked deep inside my heart.

GYS 2095 (MISCELLANEOUS) On "A Distant View of the Sea"

15
Out on the waves
   the last rays of the evening sun
      shimmer for a moment,
but that far little island
   is already in darkness.

GYS 2220 (MISCELLANEOUS) "Mountain Hut in Wind"

16
Wind from the mountain
   blows over my bamboo fence—
and goes on its way;
then from the pines on the peak
   it echoes once again.

17
The sun is almost down
   when on the horizon's edge
      something new appears:
deep back in the hazy hills,
a still more distant peak.

18
The scent of plum flowers
   fills my bedchamber;
a warbler's* song
   opens my window shutters
      to the first light of dawn.

* *Uguisu.* A bird whose song is one of the harbingers of spring.

19
With a sudden gust,
the wind blew through the trees
   and then died away.
What blossoms it left behind
   now flutter down in peace.

20
The sadness in things*
    is something with no color—
as when at nightfall
    autumn comes floating by
        on plumes of miscanthus.†[6]

* *Awaresa.* A term referring to the sadness that adheres in things perceived by those with a sensibility attuned to the perishability of human experience.
† *Obana.* Another name for flowering miscanthus (*hana susuki*), a large plant resembling pampas grass that flowers each autumn in hills and fields.

FGS 564 (AUTUMN) On the topic "Autumn Rain," written when people were composing poems on topics from *The Six Volumes of Poetry** during the time of Retired Emperor Fushimi

21
Out in the garden
    the bugs have stopped their chirping
        on this rainy night—
but from the wall comes the sound
    of a single cricket.

* *Kokin waka rokujō.* A large collection of poems from *Man'yōshū*, *Kokinshū*, and *Gosenshū*, arranged by thematic and lexical categories. Used as a primer and handbook by poets.

22

Starting, then stopping,
the hail moves through my garden
    all at a slant;
shining* banks of cloud
    darken in the sky above.

* Some commentators take this phrase *(iro naru)* as meaning "many colored."

FGS 855 (WINTER) "Evening Snow"

23

Until darkness fell
    they were at times blown clean—
those leaves on the bamboo;
but now that the wind has died
    they are left covered with snow.

FGS 915 (TRAVEL) On "Travel," from a fifty-poem sequence

24

With night coming on,
I hurry toward the hills—
eyes set on my goal:
those pines now barely tinted
    by light from the setting sun.

Kyōgoku Tamekane   105

FGS 926 (TRAVEL) Written when he was about to cross Yasukawa* ["Easy River"] while on a trip to the East Country†

25

Easy River, they call it—
but by what current of events
     did it gain that name?
Rough rapids are all I have known
     in this world of ours.[7]

* A river in Ōmi (on the border between modern Shiga and Mie Prefectures), just east of Kyōto.
† Azuma. A term referring in a general way to the provinces east of Kyōto, here more specifically to the area around Kamakura, seat of the shogunal government at the time.

FGS 929 (TRAVEL) Written when he was on the road to the East Country

26

At Takase Mountain*
     I make my way down the road
          beneath the tall pines;
an evening storm starts up,
and I meet not a soul.

* A mountain on the border between Mikawa and Tōtomi (modern Aiichi and Shizuoka Prefectures).

RW (WINTER) From among his Snow poems

27
Moon in the garden;
and on the branches, the shapes
    of cherry blossoms—
it looks the image of spring,
this dawn on a snowy day.

RW (WINTER) From a hundred-poem sequence composed at the imperial palace

28
So much more forlorn
    than its form half-concealed
in the spreading mists
    is the moor in dawn's dim light
held captive by winter frost.

NOTES

1. Quoted in Iwasa 1984:82.
2. An allusive variation on MYS 4139, by Ōtomo no Yakamochi (718–785) "The spring garden / is aglow with the deep pink / of peach blossoms — / and below, in their soft light, / a girl pausing on her way." (*Haru no sono / kurenai niou / momo no hana / shita teru michi ni / idetatsu otome.*)
3. Tamekane's preference for spring dawns echoes the tastes of the Heian lady Sei Shōnagon (964–?). See Morris 1967, 1:1.
4. In presenting a traveler who wants to stay on the road at night, Tamekane is playing his poem off against any number of earlier travel poems that show the traveler as a forlorn figure looking forward to the comfort of his inn.

5. I have taken the speaker here to be a woman, following Iwasa Miyoko (*Waka no kaishaku to kanshō jiten*, p. 489). Toki Zenmaro 1971:40–41, however, takes the speaker to be a man.

6. An allusion to SKKS 361, by Monk Jakuren (1139–1202) [Headnote: Topic unknown]: "Ah, solitude— / it is not the sort of thing / that has a color. / Mountains lined with black pine / on an evening in autumn." (*Sabishisa wa / sono iro to shi mo / nakarikeri / maki tatsu yama no / aki no yūgure.*)

7. A possible allusion to GYS 1135, by Nun Abutsu. See poem 2 in the section on Nun Abutsu in this anthology.

JAPANESE TEXTS

1 Ogi no ha o / yoku yoku mireba / ima zo shiru / tada ōki naru / susuki narikeri

2 Kyō yori wa / haru to wa shirinu / shikari tote / kinō ni kawaru / koto wa shimo nashi

3 Tori no ne mo / nodokeki yama no / asaake ni / kasumi no iro wa / haru mekinikeri

4 Ume no hana / kurenai niou / yūgure ni / yanagi nabikite / haruzame zo furu

5 Omoisomeki / yotsu no toki ni wa / hana no haru / haru no uchi ni mo / akebono no sora

6 Meguriyukaba / haru ni wa mata mo / au totemo / kyō no koyoi wa / ato ni mo araji

7 Eda ni moru / asahi no kage no / sukunaki ni / suzushisa fukaki / take no oku kana

8 Kokoro tomete / kusaki no iro mo / nagame okan / omokage ni dani / aki ya nokoru to

9 Neya no ue wa / tsumoreru yuki ni / oto mo sede / yokogiru arare / mado tataku nari

10 Konoha naki / munashiki eda ni / toshi kurete / mata megumu beki / haru zo chikazuku

11 Tomaru beki / yado o ba tsuki ni / akugarete / asu no michi yuku / yowa no tabibito

12 Hito mo tsutsumi / ware mo kasanete / toigatami / tanomeshi yowa wa / tada fuke zo yuku

13 Oriori no / kore ya kagiri mo / iku omoi / sono aware o ba / shiru hito mo nashi

14 Koto no ha ni / ideshi urami wa / tsukihatete / kokoro ni komoru / usa ni narinuru

15 Nami no ue ni / utsuru yūhi no / kage wa aredo / tōtsu kojima
wa / iro kurenikeri

16 Yamakaze wa / kakio no take ni / fukisutete / mine no matsu yori /
mata hibiku nari

17 Shizumihatsuru / irihi no kiwa ni / arawarenu / kasumeru yama no
/ nao oku no mine

18 Ume ga ka wa / makuri ni michite / uguisu no / koe yori akuru /
mado no shinonome

19 Hitoshikiri / fukimadashitsuru / kaze wa yamite / sasowanu hana
mo / nodoka ni zo chiru

20 Awaresa mo / sono iro to naki / yūgure no / obana ga sue ni / aki
zo ukaberu

21 Niwa no mushi wa / nakitomarinuru / ame no yo no / kabe ni oto
suru / kirigirisu kana

22 Furiharuru / niwa no arare wa / katayorite / iro naru kumo zo / sora
ni kureyuku

23 Kururu made / shibashi wa harau / take no ha ni / kaze wa
yowarite / yuki zo furishiku

24 Me ni kakete / kurenu ka to isogu / yamamoto no / matsu no yūhi
no / iro zo sukunaki

25 Yasukawa to / ikade ka na ni wa / nagareken / kurushiki se nomi /
aru yo to omou ni

26 Takaseyama / matsu no shitamichi / wakeyukeba / yūarashi fukite /
au hito mo nashi

27 Niwa wa tsuki / kozue wa hana no / omokage ni / haru
mekikayou / yuki no akebono

28 Kiri ni mishi / omokage yori mo / sabishiki wa / shimo ni
komoreru / nobe no akebono

Kyōgoku Tameko (d. 1316?)

Kyōgoku Tamekane was aided in all his literary endeavors by his older sister Tameko—not to be confused with another, less excellent poet of the same name who was a daughter of Nijō Tameyo. Of Tameko's official career we know little except that she began her court service in the quarters of Ōmiya'in, consort to Emperor Go-Saga and mother to both Go-Fukakusa and Kameyama, the imperial brothers whose competition over the royal succession resulted in the Jimyō-In and Daikakuji lines. Later, she also served Tamekane's great protector, Emperor Fushimi (1265–1317), as lady-in-waiting to his empress, the woman known to history as Eifuku Mon'in (1271–1342). That Tameko eventually was granted Junior Second rank and became wet-nurse to Prince Tomihito (later Emperor Hanazono) is one measure of the affection and trust which she earned in Fushimi's household.

Poetry being one area in which men and women of rank were both encouraged to excel, Tameie tutored Tameko along with her brother. In later life she was a regular participant in Jimyō-In poetry contests and gatherings, with a reputation for originality in keeping with her family background—especially in her love poems, whose musing, cerebral qualities represented a break from the sometimes subtle but more often merely quaint and precious works of the Nijō school.

Poems

GYS 440 (SUMMER) A Summer poem

1
To the sound of the wind
   it adds the refreshing notes
     of its own cool voice:
a stream down in the valley
   in the shade of the dusky hills.

GYS 1005 (WINTER) From among her Winter poems

2
Following the wind,
hail falls in a sudden burst—
passing quickly by;
then again, from between the clouds,
spills light from the moon.

GYS 1202 (TRAVEL) On "Rain at Evening in the Fields"

3

The sheets of rain
    are pushed near horizontal
by the evening wind
    that blows the straw raincoat*
of a wayfarer in the fields.

* *Mino*. A longcoat of woven straw worn by men on the road.

GYS 1292 (LOVE) From among her Love poems

4

You heartless man,
if this is the way with you
    then please teach me too—
how it is you harden your heart
    against tender feelings of love.

GYS 1535 (LOVE) A Love poem

5

In sad revery
    I abandoned my writing brush
        to its own vain whims—
and found that it had written
    just what was in my heart.

6
On the fine new robes
   people put on in the spring—
that's where first appear
   the colors of the flowers
     late in coming to the trees.

GYS 2015 (MISCELLANEOUS) At a time when something was troubling her, she went off on a pilgrimage. Looking out over a riverbed along the way, she saw clouds coming down from the peaks and the river mist rising to meet them, obscuring the pathway before her.

7
Clouds from the peak
   descend to meet the river mist
     rising from below,
leaving not a place unclouded—
just like my state of mind.

GYS 2184 (MISCELLANEOUS) "Pines Along the Coast"

8
The sky over the waves
   is hazy with falling rain;
but in the offing
   the pines out on the sand spit
     still remain in view.

GYS 2252 (MISCELLANEOUS) On the idea of "Seclusion," from a hundred-poem sequence

> 9
> In the pines, a storm;
> in the dew on the weeds,*
> the light of the moon—
> and outside of these
>   not a visitor in sight.

* *Asaji*. Cogon grass—a short reed-like plant that grows in clumps on moorlands and meadows. In poetry, it carries a melancholy connotation and is generally shown thriving around run-down or abandoned homes.

GYS 2586 (MISCELLANEOUS) Topic unknown

> 10
> Mankind and man's world:
> think on them and you wonder—
> how many ages,
> how many changes have brought us
>   to this moment we call "now?"

FGS 745 (WINTER) Topic unknown

> 11
> Showers are falling
>   from one bank moving fast,
> ahead of the rest;
> throughout the rest of the sky
>   the clouds are still calm.

FGS 1069 (LOVE) On "Waiting for Love"

> 12
> "I can't come tonight,
> but tomorrow without fail . . ."
> —the same old excuse.
> How many times must I hear it?
> How many nights must I wait?

FGS 1188 (LOVE) From among her Love poems

> 13
> So worn out with worry,
> you mustn't go to him, heart:
> stay out of his dreams!
> For even there I fear
>   he will hate me in the end.

14

This is loneliness:
the fallen paulownia* leaves
    at one with the wind—
and thus no one makes a sound
    outside my door at evening.[1]

* *Kiri.* A deciduous tree of the figwort family with large, fan-shaped yellow leaves that carpet the ground around the tree in autumn, announcing any visitor as they are trod underfoot.

FGS 1683 (MISCELLANEOUS) From among her Miscellaneous poems

15

In their seasons
    both blossoms and crimson leaves
        have times of glory;
but how moving it is to think
    that the moon never changes.

FGS 1722 (MISCELLANEOUS) Written on her way to Hie Shrine,* when
she saw the Pine of Kara Cape†

16
Out on Kara Cape
  one can see only dimly
    the sand on the beach—
but still unmistakable
  is that solitary pine.

* A shrine located at the eastern foot of Mt. Hiei, in Ōmi (modern
Shiga Prefecture), near the shore of Lake Biwa.
† Karasaki. A point on the southwest shore of Lake Biwa famous for
a solitary pine that stood there from ancient times.

FGS 1892 (MISCELLANEOUS) Topic unknown

17
Even my own heart
  is refusing to behave
    as I want it to.
So what sense would there be
  in staying angry with him?

18
Even at its longest
    man's life in this world of ours
is like a moment
    spent within a dream—
and not a long one at that.

NOTES

1. An echo of SKKS 534, by Princess Shikishi (d. 1201) [Headnote: An Autumn poem, composed for a hundred-poem sequence]: "The paulownia leaves / are hard to make a way through, / so thick have they fallen. / And yet I cannot believe / that they too wait for him to come." (*Kiri no ha mo / fumiwakegataku / narinikeri / kanarazu hito o / matsu to nakeredo.*)

JAPANESE TEXTS

1   Kaze no oto ni / suzushiki koe o / awasu nari / yūyamakage no / tani no shitamizu

2   Kaze no nochi / arare hitoshikiri / furisugite / mata murakumo ni / tsuki zo morikuru

3   Ame no ashi mo / yokosama ni naru / yūkaze ni / mino fukase yuku / nobe no tabibito

4   Uki hito yo / ware ni mo saraba / oshienan / aware o shiranu / kokorozuyosa o

5   Mono omoeba / hakanaki fude no / susabi ni mo / kokoro ni nitaru / koto zo kakaruru

6   Morobito no / haru no koromo ni / mazu zo miyuru / kozue ni osoki / hana no iroiro

7   Mine kudaru / kumo ni tachisou / kawagiri no / haruru kata naki / waga omoi kana

8   Nami no ue wa / ame ni kasumite / nagameyaru / oki no shirasu ni / matsu zo nokoreru

9 Matsu ni arashi / asaji ga tsuyu ni / tsuki no kage / sore yori hoka ni / tou hito wa nashi

10 Hito mo yo mo / omoeba aware / iku mukashi / iku utsuri shite / ima ni nariken

11 Shigureyuku / tada hitomura wa / hayaku shite / nabete no sora wa / kumo zo nodokeki

12 Sawari areba / nochi kanarazu no / nagusame yo / ikutabi kikite / ikuyo matsuran

13 Omoitsukusu / kokoro yo yukite / yume ni miyu na / so o dani hito no / itoi mo zo suru

14 Sabishisa yo / kiri no ochiba wa / kaze ni narite / hito wa oto senu / yado no yūgure

15 Toki arite / hana mo momiji mo / hito sakari / aware ni tsuki no / itsumo kawaranu

16 Karasaki ya / kasuka ni miyuru / masagochi ni / magau iro naki / hitomoto no matsu.

17 Kokoro dani / waga omou ni mo / kanawanu ni / hito o uramimu / kotowari zo naki

18 Hito no yo wa / hisashi to iu mo / hitotoki no / yume no uchi nite / sa mo hodo mo naki

Jūsammi Chikako (fl. ca. 1290–1310)

Although raised by Kitabatake Morochika (d. 1315), the lady known now as Chikako of the Junior Third rank (also referred to by the Chinese reading of her name, Shinshi) seems in fact to have been the daughter of the latter's elder brother, Tomouji (d. 1275).[1] Whatever the case, she came from a fine aristocratic family, descended from the courtly Murakami Genji.

Due chiefly to the reputation of Tameko's nephew Kitabatake Chikafusa (1293–1354), a Southern loyalist during the war between the Southern and Northern courts and the author of an important historical chronicle, the Kitabatake clan is remembered today not for poetry but for scholarship. However, recent research has shown that Chikako's father was a prominent poet in his time; and her brother Tomoaki was, like Chikako herself, an active member of Emperor Fushimi's salon.[2]

Chikako entered Fushimi's service when he was still Crown Prince, and, so far as we know, stayed on there for the rest of her life. Along with a several others in his coterie, she is now considered one of the major representatives of the Kyōgoku style.

NOTES

1. The theory is Tamai Kōsuke's. See Iwasa 1984:27.
2. Iwasa 1984:23–69.

Poems

GYS 61 (SPRING) From among her Spring poems

> 1
> In dawn's first light,
> the wind from my window
>   strikes with a chill;
> but wait, it must be spring—
> for I catch the scent of plum.*

* Along with the warbler's call and hazy skies, the advent of plum blossoms was greeted as a harbinger of spring.

GYS 1509 (LOVE) Topic unknown

> 2
> "I long for you!"—
> the words are so familiar.
> But even when they are
>   no more than a convenient lie,
> how I love to hear them!

3

Off in front of me
  on that distant summit
    is the setting sun,
while in the mountain shadow
  darkness moves through the pines.

GYS 2341 (MISCELLANEOUS) Written when the world was full of troubles*

4

Someone passes on
  and "the pity, the pity,"
we say, and say again;
no one stays for long,
and the path is hard alone.

* Referring, no doubt, to one of the military conflicts of the time.

GYS 2491 (MISCELLANEOUS) Written when she was at her old home, looking at the moon with many things on her mind

5

Not even the moon
  wants to shine very long
    in a place like this.
Outside my reed blinds
  its light is falling away.

On "Spring Rain"

6

In front of my eyes
    the drops* falling from my eaves
        swell and multiply—
and yet not a sound is made
    by the spring rain in my garden.

* Referring to her tears.

A Spring poem

7

Violets are in bloom
    in the grass along the road,
where blossoms are falling;
haze gathers in the distance
    on the fields at nightfall.

One of her Love poems

8

He made no promise
    that he would come without fail
        this very next night—
but still I am left waiting,
still I am left sad at heart.

9

Outside my window
   the peak beyond my eaves
      begins to brighten;
rising up from the valley
   comes a cloud in dawn's light.

10

In the valley shade
   smoke from fires of scrub oak
      looks thick and black;
the vespers bell* rings darkly
   on the path below the hills.

* *Iriai no kane.* Rung at temples each evening at around 6 P.M.

11

I sit idly here
   in the forlorn shadows
      of a mountain dusk—
my heart confronted
   by a single pine.[1]

From among her Buddhist poems

12
It was long ago
   that I sent my heart away
      toward the west.*
Now won't you take my body too—
O moon† on the mountain rim?[2]

* Referring to the "western paradise" of Amidist Buddhism, to which those relying upon the mercy of Amida would go after death.
† The moon was often used as a symbol of Buddhist enlightenment—a bright light shining in darkness.

NOTES

1. An echo of SKKS 1674, by Monk Saigyō. See note 1 in the section on Reizei Tamesuke in this anthology.
2. An allusive variation on SIS 1342, by Izumi Shikibu [Headnote: A poem sent to His Holiness Shōku]: "From one darkness / into another darkness / I soon must go—/ light the long way before me / moon on the mountain rim!" *Kuraki yori / kuraki michi ni zo / irinu beki / haruka ni terase / yama no ha no tsuki.*)

JAPANESE TEXTS

1 Asaake no / mado fuku kaze wa / samukeredo / haru ni wa are ya / ume ga ka zo suru
2 Omou chō / sono koto no ha yo / toki no ma no / itsuwari nite mo / kiku koto mogana
3 Ochikata no / mukai no mine wa / irihi nite / kage naru yama no / matsu zo kureyuku
4 Sakidatsu o / aware aware to / ii iite / tomaru hito naki / michi zo kanashiki

5 Shibashi dani / koko o ba tsuki mo / sumiuku ya / sudare no soto ni / kage ochite yuku

6 Miru mama ni / noki no shizuku wa / masaredomo / oto ni wa tatenu / niwa no harusame

7 Sumire saku / michi no shibafu ni / hana chirite / ochikata kasumu / nobe no yūgure

8 Kanarazu to / sa shi mo tanomenu / yūgure o / ware machikanete / ware zo kanashiki

9 Mado chikaki / nokiba no mine wa / akesomete / tani yori noboru / akatsuki no kumo

10 Tanikage ya / mashiba no keburi / koku miete / iriai kuraki / yama no shitamichi

11 Tsurezure to / yamakage sugoki / yūgure no / kokoro ni mukau / matsu no hitomoto

12 Kokoro o ba / kanete nishi ni zo / okurinuru / waga mi o sasoe / yama no ha no tsuki

Emperor Fushimi (1265–1317)

Just as one cannot speak of the Shinkokin era without mention of Retired Emperor Go-Toba, one cannot speak of the age of the *Gyokuyōshū* without giving attention to Emperor Fushimi— for without the latter's patronage it is doubtful that the accomplishments of that age would ever have been realized.

Emperor Fushimi was born to a minor consort of his father, Emperor Go-Fukakusa (1243–1304; r. 1246–1259), and thus spent his youth relatively free of the usual encumbrances of one of his status. An affable young man, he devoted himself to scholarship and the arts, especially poetry and its sister art, calligraphy. When political events made him Crown Prince he was already in his teens; and his tenure as emperor did not begin until he was an adult of twenty-three years. In the meantime, he gathered around him a cadre of young, free-spirited poets, including not only Tamekane and his sister, but a score of lesser figures and his chief consort, Shōshi, who also became a major poetic figure. His court was thus a lively one from early on, and it continued so throughout his reign (1287–1298).

Fushimi of course spent some years out of power, when Dai-kakuji rivals had control of the government. The years 1301 to 1308, comprising the reign of Go-Nijō, a supporter of the Nijō cause, were particularly difficult. That emperor's unexpected death in 1308, however, put Fushimi, now with the title Retired Emperor, back in power as the father of the reigning emperor, Hanazono (1297–1348). It was at this time that he and Tamekane, over the protests of Nijō Tameyo, conceived the idea of an imperial anthology designed to represent their new style. In 1313 the work was completed under the title *Gyokuyōshū*. With 2,796 poems, it was the largest of all imperial collections. Needless to say, it favored the Teika of the *Shin kokinshū* and the fresh, energetic approach of Fushimi's salon.

The Retired Emperor took the tonsure in 1313, and although he experienced great sorrow at the time of Tamekane's exile several years later, his last years were peaceful. His chief consort, Shōshi, was with him until his death and kept his memory alive for years to come, years in which his openness and breadth of vision found little place at court.

Writing more than a century after his death, the poet Shōtetsu compared Fushimi's calligraphy to a "withered tree, totally without outward beauty"—words of praise from one who believed in the medieval aesthetic of *sabi*, "austere beauty" *(Shōtetsu monogatari*, *NKBT* 65:167–168, 200–201). His poems too are in a spare yet intimate and melancholy style that seems to foreshadow the era of his heirs as represented in the *Fūgashū* (Collection of Elegance, 1346), a collection in which he is represented by more poems than any other poet.

Poems

One of three poems on the topic "Waiting for the Cuckoo"

1
So many nights
    have I expected your song,
o cuckoo,*
that I feel I knew your voice
    without hearing it at all.

* *Hototogisu*. A small bird of the cuckoo family whose call was believed to announce the arrival of summer.

GYS 712 (AUTUMN) Written on the night of the fifteenth day of the Eighth Month,* when he asked poets to compose fifteen-poem sequences on "The Moon"

2
The hour grew late,
yet so intent was my gaze
    I didn't know it—
until I saw so little left
    of the sky west of the moon.[1]

* The night of the full moon in the lunar calendar.

GYS 713 (AUTUMN) "The Moon at Dawn"

3

Has dawn come so soon?
The grass I trampled before
    is white with dew
when I return through the fields
    after a night with the moon.

GYS 993 (WINTER) On "Snow," from among his Winter poems

4

Pure with starlight,
the midnight sky clears
    after a light snow;
high in the tops of the trees
    I hear the passing wind.

GYS 1390 (LOVE) "Waiting for Love"

5

Come to me tonight—
and if all your promises
    on nights to come
should turn out to be lies,
then let them be lies.

GYS 1493 (LOVE) "Love, with Boat as an Image"

> 6
> In a hidden bay
>   an abandoned boat lies rotting
>   against the shoreline—
> just as my heart lies broken
>   out of yearning for you.

GYS 1798 (LOVE) From among his Love poems

> 7
> True, he may hear
>   that I am still in the world,
> living as before—
> but who is there to tell him
>   I still yearn for his love?

GYS 1887 (MISCELLANEOUS) From among his Spring poems

> 8
> I shall not forget—
> when through gaps in the blossoms
>   near the royal steps*
> it shone through thick haze—
>   the moon above the clouds.[2]

---

* *Mihashi*. The southern steps leading into the Shishinden, main ceremonial building of the residential compound of the imperial palace.

9

Is the hour that late?
The houses I pass on my way
   are all quiet now
and on the moonlit night-path
   I meet not a soul.

10

Echoing high
   in the tops of the pine trees,
it comes tumbling down
   until in the grass its voice dies—
the wind below the mountain slope.

11

Late into the night
   the moon is hazing over;
water is dripping
   into a tree-shaded pond
     where frogs are croaking.

12

Cooled down at last,
the crowds have gone back inside
   and left the night still;
the hour is late, and white
   is the path beneath the moon.

FGS 531 (AUTUMN) From among the poems of a hundred-poem sequence

13

In morning's first light
   the gaps in the clouds of mist
      show only glimpses:
how many flocks are there
   of geese* passing through the sky?[3]

* In autumn, wild geese return from Siberia to winter in Japan.

FGS 798 (WINTER) Written on the idea of "A Winter Evening"

14

An evening windstorm
   blows by in the treetops;
under a cold sun,
through clouds that portend snow—
the wild geese cry by in flight.

From among his many Love poems

15

In the midst of love
   I see one thing in everything
      within my gaze:
not a tree, not a blade of grass
   but is a vision of you.

FGS 1388 (LOVE) A Love poem

16

You—bird flying off
   into the evening sky:
not so long ago
   I too was hurrying away
      to the same place every night.

FGS 1456 (MISCELLANEOUS) On the topic "Lament in Spring"

17

Those tender feelings
   brought forth by blossoms and birds
      are mere diversions:
as I feel it in my heart
   spring is a time of pain.

18

My gaze comes to rest
    on the far mountain rim
        as nightfall begins.
Then, unlistened for, it comes—
the sound of the vespers bell.*

* *Iriai no kane*. Rung at temples each evening at around 6 P.M.

FGS 1736 (MISCELLANEOUS) On the idea of "Pines at Evening"

19

Now I have felt it—
something that exceeds storm winds
    in moving the heart:
nightfall on a mountain
    when the pines make no sound.

Written when he was having people write
poems on topics from the *Six Volumes of Poetry**

20

These rocks and trees
　　have not been given their forms
　　　　by the hand of man:
　　ah, what a fine estate they make
　　　　deep back in the hills!

* *Kokin waki rokujō.* A large collection of poems from *Man'yōshū, Ko-
kinshū,* and *Gosenshū,* arranged by thematic and lexical categories. Used
as a primer and handbook by poets.

FGS 1780 (MISCELLANEOUS) "Birds at a Mountain Home"

21

From the mountain shades,
I look beyond the bamboos
　　to where the sun falls;
and throughout the grove—
the contending cries of birds.

SSZS 1643 (MISCELLANEOUS) Among a group of poems written with words from the *Man'yōshū* was one using the phrase "a crane comes flying into view"[4]

22

From the broad sea plain
    our boat rows on toward shore—
when across the beach
    laid bare by the evening tide,
a crane comes flying into view.

FG 364 (SPRING)

23

In the hazy night
    the sky seen through the trees
        seems indistinct;
rich with the scent of flowers
    are the rays of the spring moon.

NOTES

1. A possible allusion to SKKS 1536, by Monk Saigyō [Headnote: Topic unknown]: "The hour grew late / while I watched my shadow, / lamenting my old age—/ till off in the distance / the moon was about to set." (*Fukenikeru / waga mi no kage o / omou ma ni / haruka ni tsuki no / katabukinikeru.*)

2. An allusive variation on SG 2177, by Fujiwara no Teika. See poem 45 in the section on Fujiwara no Teika in this anthology.

3. An allusive variation on SZS 419, by Fujiwara no Sadayori (995–1045) [Headnote: Written when he went to Uji]: "In morning's first light / the mist on Uji River / is all breaks and gaps—/ and appearing

everywhere, / bamboo stakes of fishing weirs." (*Asaborake / uji no kawagiri / taedae ni / arawarewataru / sese no ajirogi.*)

4. A line taken from MYS 1160, anonymous: "On Naniwa Shore / I stand on the dry tideland / and look afar / as toward Awaji Isle / cranes come flying into view." (*Naniwagata / shiohi ni tachite / miwataseba / awaji no shima ni / tazu wataru miyu.*)

JAPANESE TEXTS

1 Nakinu beki / yūgure goto no / aramashi ni / kikade narenuru / hototogisu kana

2 Fukenu to mo / nagamuru hodo wa / oboenu ni / tsuki yori nishi no / sora zo sukunaki

3 Akenuru ka / waketsuru ato ni / tsuyu shiroshi / tsuki no kaesa no / nobe no michishiba

4 Hoshi kiyoki / yowa no usuyuki / sora harete / fukitōsu kaze o / kozue ni zo kiku

5 Koyoi toe ya / nochi no ikuyo wa / ikutabi no / yoshi itsuwari to / naraba naru tomo

6 Uragakure / irie ni sutsuru / warebune no / ware zo kudakete / hito wa koishiki

7 Ikite yo ni / ari to bakari wa / kikaru to mo / koishinobu to wa / tare ka tsutaemu

8 Wasurezu yo / mihashi no hana no / konoma yori / kasumite fukeshi / kumo no ue no tsuki

9 Fukenuru ka / sugiyuku yado mo / shizumarite / tsuki no yo michi ni / au hito mo mashi

10 Hibikikuru / matsu no ure yori / fukiochite / kusa ni koe yamu / yama no shita kaze

11 Sayo fukaku / tsuki wa kasumite / mizu otsuru / kokage no ike ni / kawazu naku nari

12 Susumitsuru / amata no yado mo / shizumarite / yo fukete shiroki / michinobe no tsuki

13 Asaborake / kiri no harema no / taedae ni / iku tsura suginu / amatsu karigane

14 Kozue ni wa / yūarashi fukite / samuki hi no / yukige no kumo ni / kari nakiwataru

15 Koishisa ni / naritatsu naka no / nagame ni wa / omokage naranu / kusa mo ki mo nashi

16 Tori no yuku / yūbe no sora yo / sono yo ni wa / ware mo isogishi / kata wa sadameki

17 Hana tori no / nasake wa ue no / susabi nite / kokoro no uchi no /
haru zo monouki

18 Yama no ha no / nagame ni ataru / yūgure ni / kikade kikoyuru /
iriai no oto

19 Ima shi mo wa / arashi ni masaru / aware kana / oto senu matsu
no / yūgure no yama

20 Tsukurowanu / iwaki o niwa no / sugata nite / yado mezurashiki /
yama no oku kana

21 Yamakage ya / take no anata ni / irihi ochite / hayashi no tori no /
koe zo arasou

22 Watahara ya / oki kogikureba / yūshio no / higata no ura ni / tazu
wataru miyu

23 Kasumu yo no / ko no ma no sora wa / oboro nite / hana ni
kaoreru / haru no tsukikage

Empress Eifuku (1271–1342)

When Emperor Fushimi died in 1317, so high was the esteem in which he held his wife of thirty years, the lady Eifuku Mon'in, that he left instructions to his heirs to look to his empress as a guide in matters of poetry.

A daughter of the court minister Saionji Sanekane, Eifuku Mon'in, known then as Shōshi, had come to Fushimi's chambers in 1388. Although unable to bear children, she seems always to have enjoyed the affections of the emperor, with whom she shared a consuming passion for poetry.

The decades after Fushimi's death were not easy ones for the Jimyō-In line. After being forced to retire in 1318, Emperor Hanazono came to live at the crowded family palace in northern Kyoto—along with Retired Emperor Go-Fushimi (r. 1298–1301), the latter's chief consort, and young Prince Kazuhito (1313–1364). While waiting for a change in the political climate, they bided their time with poetry and the other elegant arts. Imperial anthologies were produced by the Nijō faction in 1320 and 1326, but with little involvement from the Ex-empress' circle. In the case of the latter work, in fact, she and her supporters voiced their protest against Nijō dominance by refusing to submit any of their work to the compilers for review.

When Prince Kazuhito ascended the throne as Emperor Kōgon in 1331, Eifuku Mon'in dared once again to imagine a bright future for her wards. But the well-known rebellion of Go-Daigo in the summer of 1333 put her hopes in peril. For a time, Go-Fushimi, Hanazono, and Kōgon fled to the Rokuhara offices of the Kamakura government for safety, only to be greeted with the collapse of the Hōjō government and the beginning of Go-Daigo's Imperial Restoration. In the tumultuous days that followed, the three men barely escaped physical harm, and others were not so lucky. Saionji Kinmune, the heir of Eifuku Mon'in's parent house, was cut down on imperial order. When the Ex-empress lost Hanazono to the tonsure in 1333 and Go-Fushimi to illness in 1336, there seemed little reason to look forward to anything but lonely retirement and death.

Nevertheless, she did live to see some restitution of the Saionji fortunes and a modest revival of the Kyōgoku style—all after Go-Daigo was chased from the capital by Ashikaga Takauji in 1337. From the late 1320s she had moved from the capital proper to an old Saionji estate in Kitayama. There she held poetry meetings and looked after Saionji Sanetoshi, the heir of her family. Although she died before the compilation of *Fūgashū* (1346), she was clearly the force behind it. Knowledge of the events of her last years helps us to understand that anthology's somber tones. While Emperor Hanazono criticized her poems for being to "pretty" and lacking in directness (see Iwasa 1976:42), no one would deny her importance as one of the greatest patron-poets of the age.

Poems

GYS 196 (SPRING) "Blossom at Dawn"

1
From the mountain's base
    comes birdcall after birdcall—
bringing on the dawn;
clump after clump of blossoms
    begin to show their colors.

GYS 249 (SPRING) From among her Spring poems

2
It is the breezes
    and ever-progressing time
        that one should resent—
in the heart of the blossoms
    there is no desire to fall.[1]

3
I hear it in the wind
    and see it among the clouds
        gathering at dusk—
the relentless advance
    of autumn's melancholy.

GYS 924 (WINTER) Topic unknown

4
The river plovers*—
is the chill of the moonlit night
    keeping them awake?
Every time I start from sleep
    I hear their voices calling.[2]

* *Kawa chidori*. Small shore birds whose plaintive cry is often employed
by poets as a symbol of winter loneliness.

GYS 1382 (LOVE) On "Waiting for Love"

5
On evenings like this
    one can almost be happy
        to receive no word—
as a sign the vows still hold
    that we made the night before.

GYS 1407 (LOVE) Written as a Love poem

6

He made no promise—
so I try to tell myself
   not to be bitter
until this long night too
   ends with a lonely dawn.

GYS 1704 (LOVE) Written for a thirty-poem sequence, on the topic "Unrequited Love"

7

If even now
   in the midst of rejection
      I still love* him so,
then what would be my feelings
   if he were to love me back?

* The word used is *aware,* which usually means "pity." Here the context seems to justify translating it as "love."

GYS 2123 (MISCELLANEOUS) From a hundred-poem sequence

8

Deep into the night
   the moon sinks behind the peak,
just beyond my eaves;
from the dark cypress groves
   comes the sound of storm winds.

9

My heart is moved
    from one time to another,
unable to choose—
between blossoms, the cuckoo,
the moon, and the snow.*

* The four representing the four seasons: spring (blossoms), summer
(the cuckoo), autumn (the moon), and winter (snow).

GYS 2688 (BUDDHISM) "On the Teachings of Buddha"

10

For just a moment
    a heart has taken lodging
        in this body*—
why then this look on my face
    as if to last forever?

* According to Buddhist doctrine, the soul goes through many rein-
carnations, each as temporary as the last.

11
On cherry petals
   the rays of the setting sun
      flutter for a moment—
and then, before one knows it,
the light has faded away.[3]

FGS 478 (AUTUMN) From among her Autumn poems

12
Scattering blossoms
   from my garden bush-clover,*
the wind strikes hard;
the last rays of evening sun
   are fading from my wall.

* *Hagi*. A large shrub that produces tiny reddish-pink blossoms each autumn.

FGS 508 (AUTUMN) From among her many Autumn poems

13
The evening sunlight
   on the moss on the boulder
      has faded away;
in the willows on the hill,
an autumn wind is blowing.

FGS 1046 (LOVE) Written as a Love poem

14
The night has fallen.
If only on those high clouds
    flying through the sky
I could send this question:
"Where will you be tonight?"

FGS 1069 (LOVE) On "Waiting in Secret for Love"

15
Even the night wind
    banging my open pine door
is an unkind sound
    when I wait in secret hope
late into the night.[4]

FGS 1141 (LOVE) From among her Love poems

16
I got used to him—
and was gradually drawn along
    by a growing fondness,
until now the time has come
    that I can hate him no more.

Written as a Love poem

17

In the whole wide world
    there is no place to find rest,
no place to find love.
Where can this body of mine
    gain even a moment's peace?

From among her Miscellaneous poems

18

In just the same way
    yesterday came to its end,
the sun going down
    behind the crest of the hill—
and then the voices of the bells.*

* *Kane no koegoe.* Vespers bells, rung at temples each evening at around
6 P.M.

Eifuku mon'in hyakuban go-jika-awase, round 26

19

An evening shower
    leaves not a cloud behind it
        in the clear sky;
climbing up my bamboo blinds
    come the rays of the night moon.

From *Tōza uta-awase*[5]

20
Has the new day dawned?
Realizing that tonight
 I am alone again,
I gaze at the torchlight
 glowing in my tears.

NOTES

1. An allusive variation on GSS 92, by Kiyowara no Fukayabu (tenth century) [Headnote: Topic unknown]: "Like a long rope, / spring stretches out so slowly / in apparent calm. / What in the heart of the blossoms / makes them hurry things along?" (*Uchihaete / haru wa sabakari / nodokeki o / hana no kokoro ya / nani isoguran.*)

2. An echo of SIS 224, by Ki no Tsurayuki [Headnote: Topic unknown]: "Overcome by love, / I go out in pursuit of her— / the river wind / so cold in the winter night / that the plovers cry." (*Omoikane / imogari yukeba / fuyu no yo no / kawakaze sumumi / chidori naku nari.*)

3. An echo of GYS 2095, by Kyōgoku Tamekane. See poem 15 in the section on Kyōgoku Tamekane in this anthology.

4. A possible allusion to GSIS 920, by Izumi Shikibu [Headnote: Sent to a man who said he would come but then didn't, making her wait in vain all night]: "I held off, hoping— / and did not even pull shut / my door of black pine. Why then am I now seeing dawn / end a winter night?" (*Yasurai ni / maki no to koso wa / sasazarame / ika ni akenuru / fuyu no yo naran.*)

5. From a poem contest. Quoted in Tsugita 1976.

JAPANESE TEXTS

1 Yamamoto no / tori no koegoe / akesomete / hana mo muramura / iro zo mieyuku

2   Sugiutsuru / toki to kaze to zo / urameshiki / hana no kokoro wa / chiramu to mo seji

3   Kaze ni kiki / kumo ni nagamuru / yūgure no / aki no uree zo / taezu nariyuku

4   Kawa chidori / tsukiyo o samumi / inezu are ya / nezamuru goto ni / koe no kikoyuru

5   Oto senu ga / ureshiki ori mo / arikeru yo / tanomi sadamete / nochi no yūgure

6   Tanomeneba / hito ya wa yuki to / omoinasedo / koyoi mo tsui ni / mata akenikeri

7   Kaku bakari / uki ga ue dani / aware nari / aware nariseba / ikaga aramashi

8   Sayo fukaki / nokiba no mine ni / tsuki wa irite / kuraki hibara ni / arashi o zo kiku

9   Kokoro utsuru / nasake izure to / wakikanenu / hana hototogisu / tsuki yuki no toki

10 Karisome ni / kokoro no yado to / nareru mi o / aru monogao ni / nani omouramu

11 Hana no ue ni / shibashi utsurou / yūzukuhi / iru to mo nashi ni / kage kienikeri

12 Mahagi chiru / niwa no akikaze / mi ni shimite / yūhi no kage zo / kabe ni kieyuku

13 Yūzukuhi / iwane no koke ni / kage kiete / oka no yanagi wa / akikaze zo fuku

14 Kurenikeri / ama tobu kumo no / yukiki ni mo / koyoi ika ni to / tsutae teshigana

15 Maki no to o / kaze no narasu mo / ajiki nashi / hito shirenu yo no / yaya fukuru hodo

16 Naruru ma no / aware ni tsui ni / hikarekite / itoigataku zo / ima wa narinuru

17 Ōkata no / yo wa yasuge nashi / hito wa ushi / waga mi izuku ni / shibashi okamashi

18 Kaku shite zo / kinō mo kureshi / yama no ha no / irihi no nochi ni / kane no koegoe

19 Yūdachi no / kumo mo nokorazu / sora harete / sudare o noboru / yoi no tsukikage

20 Akenuru ka / mata koyoi mo to / omou yori / namida ni ukabu / tomoshibi no kage

DIVIDED RANKS

Nijō Tameyo

Tonna

Yoshida no Kenkō

Jōben

Nijō Tamesada

Keiun

Emperor Hanazono

Emperor Kōgon

Reizei Tamehide

Nijō Tameshige

Nijō Yoshimoto

Prince Munenaga

Nijō Tameyo (1250–1338)

As the senior heirs of the Mikohidari house, the family of Tame-
uji was known in his time by the clan name of Fujiwara. It was
only later, in the days of Tameuji's heir, Tameyo, that they came
to be known as the Nijō—a name taken, as was the custom of
the time, from the area of Kyōto where the primary residence of
the family was located.

In his teens, Tameyo studied under his grandfather Tameie;
later he looked to his father as a tutor as well. By his twenties
he was already a prominent poet, and he maintained his position
most of his life despite political conflicts involving the imperial
family that made his career one of decided ups and downs. Af
filiated with the Daikakuji line from early on, he gathered honors
and appointments during their administrations; when the Jimyō-
In emperors held sway, he withdrew into unhappy seclusion.
Notwithstanding these misfortunes, he eventually rose to the usual
position of Mikohidari heirs, Minister of Popular Affairs and Major
Counselor of Senior Second rank.

During periods of Daikakuji ascendancy, Tameyo was a busy
man, acting as sole compiler of the *Shin gosenshū* (New Later
Collection) from 1301 to 1303, and again in the same role for
the *Shoku senzaishū* (Collection of a Thousand Years Continued)
from 1318 to 1320. His prosperity continued into the reign of
the energetic and ambitious Go-Daigo (r. 1318–1339), another
heir of the Daikakuji line and a great patron of the arts. When
an order for an imperial anthology came once more in the early

1320s, he could have taken the compiler's honors for himself, but instead declined in favor of his son Tamefuji (1275–1324).

Tameyo took the tonsure in 1329, at the age of seventy-nine, hoping to spend his last years in peace. Little did he know that civil war would begin just a few years later, and at the instigation of his patron Go-Daigo. When his protector was exiled by the Kamakura shogunate and later driven from the capital by Ashikaga troops that would set up a new military government, Tameyo kept his own counsel. At the time of his death in the autumn of 1338, the fate of the Daikakuji line was still unsure.

One of Tameyo's legacies was his many students—including his own sons and grandsons and a group of monk-poets known as the Four Deva Kings of Poetry[1] who would dominate poetic affairs for the next half-century. His other legacy was what came to be known as Nijō philosophy, which he articulated in *Waka teikin* (A Primer for Poets, 1326?). Among other things, he interpreted Teika's maxim "old words, new heart" to mean only old words of a decorous nature and only a new heart of courtly elegance.[2] His conservative "refinements" of his great-grandfather's pronouncements defined the direction of Nijō poetics for generations to come.

NOTES

1. Named after four Indian gods (*shitennō*) who protected the four corners—east, west, north, and south—from demons. At first the list of poets included Tonna, Kenkō, Jōben, and an obscure figure named Nōyo who was later replaced by Jōben's son, Keiun.
2. *NKT* 4:115–118. See introduction to this anthology, pp. 5–6.

Poems

SGSS 151 (SPRING) Written when the senior courtiers were composing on the topic "Dawn Moon in Late Spring," at a time when the Retired Emperor was still on the throne.

> 1
> O moon at dawn,
> prolonging your stay in the sky
>   with such indifference—
> won't you teach your ways to spring
>   before it draws to a close?[1]

SGSS 1493 (MISCELLANEOUS) After Taira no Sadatoki took the tonsure, Tameyo heard that Nobutoki too had left the world. He sent them this poem.

> 2
> That just one of you
>   had cast aside the world's cares
>   was cause for sadness.
> And now I hear with greater grief
>   that you have retired together.

On "Day After Day of Snow," presented as part of a thirty-poem sequence

3

Now even the sound
   of the bamboo shafts breaking
      has come to an end—
so deep have the drifts become
   after days and days of snow.

GYS 2205 (MISCELLANEOUS) On "Mountain Home," from *The Hundred-Poem Sequences of the Kagen Era* [1303]*

4

Because this village
   sits in the mountain's shadow,
it rings later here,
   well after night has fallen—
      the sound of the vespers bell.†

* Referring to a number of such sequences commissioned from Tameyo and others by Retired Emperor Go-Uda in preparation for the compilation of the *Shin gosenshū*.
† *Iriai no kane*. Rung at temples each evening around 6 p.m.

5

If I could have my way,
I would place it in the sky—
that gate of spring haze.*
There at least it might forestall
    the geese on their cloudy way.†

* *Kasumi no seki*. Toll barriers (*seki*) were placed by the government along major thoroughfares as a means of raising revenue and keeping track of movements. Here the poet uses the term metaphorically to refer to a bank of haze that he wishes would stop the geese from going away.
† The departure of wild geese for the continent was one of the few melancholy events announcing the arrival of spring.

SHOKUSZS 284 (SUMMER) On "A River at the Time of the Fifth-Month Rains"

6

In the mountain stream
    there is no crashing sound now
        of water on rock.
The waves are running high
    with rains of the Fifth Month.*

* *Samidare*. Referring to Japan's rainy season, which came during the fifth month of the lunar calendar.

SHOKUSZS 302 (SUMMER) Presented as part of *The Hundred-Poem Sequences of the Kagen Era* [1303]

7
The cormorant boats*
   are pushing their way upstream
against white waves
   that transport back downstream
the light of their fishing fires.†[2]

* Men fished at night with cormorants—large sea-ravens with banded necks that were trained to catch fish and then come back to the boat and disgorge them.
† *Kagaribi*. Fires kept burning in cauldrons on the prows of cormorant boats to attract fish at night.

SHOKUSZS 1233 (LOVE) From a fifty-poem sequence composed at the house of the Reverend Prince of the Second rank

8
What use is prayer
   if the one I pray about
      remains so heartless?
Were my prayers not answered
   I would only resent the gods.

SHOKUSZS 1413 (LOVE) On "Unrequited Love"

9
What is it
   that is senseless to lament
     after awaking?
A love pledge made in a dream
   one will never see again.[3]

SHOKUGYW (AUTUMN) On "The Moon on the Mountain," from a fifty-poem sequence composed at the house of the Reverend Prince of the Second rank

10
Not even waiting
   for the winds to sweep away
the floating clouds
   from the peak where it rises
is the emerging moon.[4]

REW (SUMMER) From a fifty-poem sequence on the moon composed at the residence of the Retired Emperor Go-Uda on the fifteenth day of the Ninth Month of the third year of the Genkō era [1323]

11
Cooler than the wind
   that has kept me waiting
is the moonlight
   shining through the one layer
of my summer robe.[5]

NOTES

1. An allusion to KKS 625, by Mibu no Tadamine. See note 2 in the section of this anthology on Fujiwara no Tameuji.

2. An allusive variation on SKKS 252, by Monk Jakuren [Headnote: Written on "Cormorant Boats" for a poem-contest of hundred-poem sequences at the home of the Regent-Chancellor]: "The cormorant boats / must have pushed their way / into the rapids— / for the light of their fishing fires / is rolling with the waves." (*Ukaibune / takase sashikosu / hodo nare ya / musubōreyuku / kagaribi no kage.*)

3. An allusive variation on KKS 609, by Mibu no Tadamine [Headnote: Topic unknown]: "Harder to accept / than the loss of life itself— / this awakening / from an uncompleted dream / where I encountered my love." (*Inochi ni mo / masarite oshiku / aru mono wa / mihatenu yume / samuru narikeri.*) McCullough 1985:137.

4. An allusive variation on SCSS 253, by the Ōinomikado Minister of the Right [Headnote: A Moon poem, sent to a poem contest held at the home of Provisional Counselor Tsunesada when the latter was still a Middle Captain]: "In the high heavens / floating clouds are swept away / by autumn winds— / showing without a shadow / the clear moon of midnight." (*Amatsu sora / ukigumo harau / akikaze ni / kuma naku sumeru / yowa no tsuki.*)

5. An allusive variation on SKKS 260, by Gokyōgoku Yoshitsune [Headnote: For a poem contest of hundred-poem sequences]: "I still feel cool / even with two layers— / one of summer robes / with another of moonlight / lodging in my thin sleeves." (*Kasanete mo / suzushikarikeri / natsugoromo usuki tamoto ni / yadoru tsukikage.*)

JAPANESE TEXTS

1 Tsurenakute / nokoru narai o / kurete yuku / haru ni oshieyo / ariake no tsuki

2 Yo o sutsuru / hitokata o koso / nagekitsure / tomo ni somuku to / kiku zo kanashiki

3 Shitaore no / take no oto sae / taehatenu / amari ni tsumoru / yuki no hikazu ni

4 Kono sato wa / yamakage nareba / hoka yori mo / kurehatete kiku / iriai no koe

5 Onajiku wa / sora ni kasumi no / seki mogana / kumoji no kari o / shibashi todomen

6 Yamakawa no / iwa ni sekaruru / oto mo nashi / ue kosu nami no / samidare no koro

7 Ukaibune / sese sashinoboru / shiranami ni / utsurite kudaru / kagaribi no kage

8 Tsure mo naki / hito o ba okite / inoru tomo / awazu wa mata ya / kami o uramin

9 Nageku to mo / samete no nochi ni / kai naki wa / mata minu yume no / chigiri narikeri

10 Yamakaze no / harau mo matade / ukigumo no / kakaru onoe o / izuru tsukikage

11 Mataretsuru / kaze yori mo nao / natsugoromo / hitoe ni tsuki no / kage zo suzushiki

Tonna (1289–1372)

Like the poet-priest Saigyō, one of the great poets of the past
to whom he looked as a model, Tonna was born into a military
family, the Nikaidō, but took the tonsure at around age twenty
and devoted the rest of his life to religion—he seems to have
been a member of the Ji sect—and the Way of Poetry. After
sojourns on Mt. Hiei and Mt. Koya and several trips to the East
Country, he became a student of Nijō Tameyo, going on there-
after to develop close relationships with all of the most important
Nijō adherents of the next half-century, including Tameyo's heirs
Tamefuji, Tamesada, Tameakira (1295–1364), Tametō (1341–
1381), and Tameshige (1325–1385). His devotion to Nijō po-
etic principles even through the hard times when the opposing
faction held sway won him the respect of the family and a lasting
place in medieval literary history. Along with three of Tameyo's
other priestly disciples—Jōben, Keiun, and Yoshida no Kenkō—
Tonna came to be known as one of the Four Deva Kings of
Poetry.[1]

It was after the death of Tameyo in 1338 that Tonna achieved
his greatest prominence as a senior poet of the Nijō tradition.
Living for most of his long life in the Eastern Hills area of the
capital at Kyōto, he acted as critic and contest judge in the salons
of the court aristocracy and of the age's military barons, including
the two shōguns Ashikaga Takauji (1305–1358) and Ashikaga
Yoshiakira (1330–1367). Since he was not of actual Nijō blood-
line, he could not hope for the public recognition afforded his
aristocratic friends, but when Nijō Tameakira died before com-

pleting the compilation of *Shin shuishū* (New Collection of Gleanings) in 1364, Tonna was granted the privilege of completing the task—the only man of such relatively low status ever to be granted such an honor.[2]

Although friendly in his later years with some Reizei poets, particularly Tamehide, Tonna's critical writings show him to be a champion of the plain style advocated by Tameyo, whose poetry he commended as a model for young poets especially. His essays typically use words such as *sunao* ("gentle, calm"), *uruwashi* ("visually beautiful"), and *akiraka* ("clear") as terms of praise.[3]

Tonna's poetry reflects his critical stance almost perfectly. Although lacking the spontaneity and adventuresome spirit of the Kyōgoku-Reizei school, his work is noteworthy for its courtly refinement, restrained lyricism, and mastery of convention qualities that made his personal anthology, *Sōanshū* (The Grass Hut Collection), a model for later generations of Nijō poets.

NOTES

1. Named after the *Shitennō*, four Indian gods who protected the four corners—east, west, north, and south—from demons.
2. Ishida 1943: 101–111.
3. See *Seiashō* and *Gumon kenchū*, in *NKT* 5.

Poems

SSZS 1718 (MISCELLANEOUS) Once, in the Third Month, Minister of Popular Affairs Tamefuji visited Tonna at his hut in the Eastern Hills* to see the cherry blossoms. After returning home Tamefuji sent this poem:

> 1
> What has become now
>   of the cherry trees
>   at your mountain home?
> On the capital's blossoms
>   the winds of spring are blowing.†

* Higashiyama. The hills on the eastern border of the capital at Kyōto.
† In the original anthology, this poem by Tamefuji is quoted in the headnote to the poem by Tonna that follows.

This was Tonna's reply:

> 2
> At my mountain home
>   your footprints have disappeared
>   from my empty garden—
> where over scattered blossoms
>   the winds of spring are blowing.

On "Spring's End in a Mountain Hut"

3

In a mountain home,
where the passing days and months
   go by unnoticed,
the blooming of the cherries
   marks the end of spring.*

* Cherries bloom later in the mountains—although the poet's statement here should no doubt be understood as representing the pose of the recluse.

From among his Laments

4

Since all things must end,
one should spend no time lamenting
   the sadness of one's fate:
all that a man should do
   is wait for old age to come.

SZKKS 1640 (MISCELLANEOUS) Written after the line "Flowers blossoming, wind and rain in abundance," when he was composing poems on lines from ancient Chinese poems

5

In this world of ours
    truly this is the way of things*—
blossoms in full bloom,
wind blowing from the mountains,
and spring rain falling.

* In other words, no sooner do the flowers bloom than nature's forces gather to blow them away.

SS 120 (SPRING) "A Lark"

6

In the spreading haze
    that moves through the sky
      I can't make it out—
the dusk-lark is only a voice
    rising up and away.[1]

ss 347 (SUMMER) On "Summer Flowers Before the Wind," written for a poem contest between young and old at the home of the Minister of Popular Affairs

7

In summer grasses
 the leaves on the reeds*
  remain unseen—
but telling us they are there
 is the passing evening wind.[2]

* *Ogi*. A large flowering grass resembling *susuki* (miscanthus) in shape and features.

ss 541 (AUTUMN) On "The Night of the Fifteenth Day of the Eighth Month," written at Konrenji* when people were "searching topics"† involving the moon

8

An old man now,
I watch the full moon tonight
 with feelings profound—
for I too have passed
 the halfway point of life.

* A temple of the Ji Sect, located north of Kyōto.
† *Dai o saguru*. An informal poem contest in which poets gathered to compose poems extemporaneously on topics written out, placed on a dais, and then chosen at random.

Written when he spent the night at a place called Kinya*

9

Has it grown so late?
Even the sounds of punt poles†
    pushing through the pools
seem to ring out more clearly
    in the light of the moon.

* Location unknown.
† Punt poles (*sao*) were used to push flatboats (*takasebune*) through pools.

Among three poems composed at the home of the Ogura Consultant and Middle Captain

10

The fields, the mountains
    all look frost-withered now;
leaving the sunlight
    shining just before nightfall
        all that's left of autumn.

On "Night Drizzle," written at the home of Master of the Palace Table Office Yoriyasu

11
Even the showers
    fall, then stop, then fall again
        in brief bursts of sound—
while I lie awake at night
    pondering the world's restless ways.[3]

SS 683 (WINTER) On "Falling Leaves," written at the house of the (posthumously named) Minister of the Left

12
The mountain wind blows
    as if it means to leave behind
not a single one
    of the dead leaves piling up
underneath the trees.[4]

SS 1052 (LOVE) From a hundred-poem sequence requested by the Mikohidari Middle Counselor

13
As swift as the moon
    passing through the gaps
        in gathering clouds—
so swift are the changes
    of the human heart.[5]

SS 1340 (LAMENTS) Written on a snowy morning when he was visiting the grave of one of his disciples.

14

Gone on before me
   is the one who should in time
      have come to my grave;
how sad to be walking now
    through the snow of this mountain road!

SS 1384 (BUDDHISM) From among his Buddhist poems

15

If in the next life
   you would rest on the calyx
      of a blossom,
then here you must make your home
    at the base of a tree.*

* Those born into the Buddhist paradise are envisioned as seated on the central calyx of a lotus blossom. Here, however, Tonna may be hinting at a more poetic, although less pious, wish: to be reborn a cherry blossom.

On "A Snipe Before the Moon," at the house of the Regent on the night of the thirteenth day of the Ninth Month

16
Up from the paddies
   where the moon has spent the night,*
a snipe leaves its roost —
rising from the icepack
   into the dawning sky.[6]

* The moon is said to "take lodging in" things that reflect its light: water, dew, and, in this case, ice.

SHOKUSS 364 (LOVE) "Waiting for Love in Vain"

17
What shall I do now?
I was waiting for the moon
   to hear my complaints,
but now the late-night sky
   has gone entirely to rain.

REW (WINTER)

18
The fields, the mountains
   look bright and clear tonight;
in the pitch blackness
   of the waking gloom of night—
a fall of white snow.

NOTES

1. An allusive variation on FGS 133, by Archbishop Jien [Headnote: From among his spring poems]: "Out in the fields / where spring lies deep in haze / a low wind passes—/ flinging a dusk-lark / up into the sky." (*Haru fukaki / nobe no kasumi no / shitakaze ni / fukarete agaru / yūhibari kana.*)

2. An allusive variation on SIS 139 (also *Shinsen waka* 8), by Ki no Tsurayuki [Headnote: Written on a standing screen during the Engi era]: "A gentle rustle / sighing through miscanthus leaves—/ the first whispered sound / startling us to awareness / of the autumn's coming." (*Ogi no ha no / soyogu oto koso / akikaze no / hito ni shiraruru / hajime narikere.*) McCullough 1985:297.

3. An echo of SKKS 1563, by the Reverend Prince Shukaku (d. 1202) [Headnote: Written on "Lamentation" when he asked people to write fifty-poem sequences]: "While the wind passes / whispering in the bamboo grass, / I lie awake / pondering the fickle world, / wet with the dew of my tears." (*Kaze soyogu / shino no ozasa no / kari no yo o / omou nezame ni / tsuyu zo koboruru.*)

4. A possible echo of ShokuSIS 397, by Fujiwara no Tameuji. See poem 5 in the section on Fujiwara no Tameuji in this anthology.

5. An echo of FGS 639, by Saionji Sanekane ([Headnote: Topic unknown]: "As swift as the moon / passing through gaps / in gathering clouds—/ so seems my own decline / amid the sadness of autumn." (*Murakumo no / hima yuku tsuki no / hayaku nomi / katabuku oi no / aki zo kanashiki.*)

6. An allusion to SKKS 362, by Monk Saigyō [Headnote: Topic unknown]: "Even one who claims / to no longer have a heart / feels this sad beauty: / a snipe flying up from a marsh / on an evening in autumn." (*Kokoro naki / mi ni mo aware wa / shirarekeri / shigi tatsu sawa no / aki no yūgure.*)

JAPANESE TEXTS

1 Yamazato no / kozue wa ikaga / narinuran / miyako no hana wa / harukaze zo fuku

2 Yamazato wa / towareshi niwa mo / ato taete / chirishiku hana ni / harukaze zo fuku

3 Utsuriyuku / tsukihi mo shiranu / yamazato wa / hana o kagiri ni / haru zo kurenuru

4   Kagiri areba / mi no uki koto mo / nagekarezu / oi o zo hito wa /
    matsubekarikeru

5   Yo no naka wa / kaku koso arikere / hanazakari / yamakaze fukite /
    harusame zo furu

6   Kasumi tatsu / sora ni wa sore to / miewakade / koe nomi agaru /
    yūhibari kana

7   Natsukusa no / shigemi ni wakanu / ogi no ha o / shirasete
    suguru / nobe no yukaze

8   Oite miru / koyoi no tsuki zo / aware naru / waga mi mo itsuka /
    nakaba nariken

9   Fukenuru ka / takase no yodo ni / sasu sao no / oto sae sumeru /
    tsuki no kage kana

10 No mo yama mo / shimogarehatete / kurenu ma no / hikage bakari
    ni / nokoru aki kana

11 Shigure sae / furimi furazumi / oto sunari / sadamenaki yo o / omou
    nezame ni

12 Ko no moto ni / tsumoru momiji o / izuku ni mo / nao nokosaji
    to / yamakaze so fuku

13 Murakumo no / hima yuku tsuki no / hayaku nomi / utsuru wa hito
    no / kokoro narikeri

14 Waga ato mo / tou beki hito wa / sakidatete / yamaji no yuki o /
    wakuru kanashisa

15 Nochi no yo no / hana no utena o / tanomu mi wa / mazu ko no
    moto zo / sumika narikeru

16 Tsuki yadoru / sawada no tsura ni / fusu shigi no / kōri yori tatsu /
    akegata no sora

17 Ika ni sen / tsuki o kaguto ni / matsu yowa no / fukeyuku sora zo
    / ame ni narinuru

18 No mo yama mo / sayaka ni miete / ubatama no / yami no utsutsu
    ni / fureru shirayuki

Yoshida no Kenkō (b. 1283)

Although now most famous as the author of *Tsurezuregusa* (Essays in Idleness),[1] a miscellany made up of anecdotes and short essays on culture and aesthetics, Yoshida no Kenkō was known chiefly as a poet in his own time. Born into a minor aristocratic family, he entered the service of Emperor Go-Nijō (r. 1301–1308) as a low-level bureaucrat when still a young man and retired from public life upon the death of his protector in 1308. He took the tonsure in 1313, spending the rest of his life as a semirecluse.

Kenkō's poetic career began rather late, well after his retirement from court life, when he became a student of Nijō Tameyo. But it did not take him long to establish himself as a major talent, earning a place for himself among the Four Deva Kings of Poetry.[2] His many known contacts with other poets—the Nijō family, military poets associated with the shogunal house, Tonna, and, in his later years, Reizei Tamehide and Imagawa Ryōshun—make it clear that he was one of the more popular men of his day. Although he left no poetic criticism per se, his comments on poetic styles in *Tsurezuregusa* reveal a generally conservative and profoundly nostalgic sensibility.

Writing only a few decades after Kenkō's death, Nijō Yoshimoto noted that already Kenkō had lost much of the fame he had enjoyed as a contemporary of Tonna, whose reputation had in contrast only grown during that same period of time.[3] One of the reasons for this seems to be that Kenkō did not excel at *hare no uta,* those formal poems written on specific topics for public occasions—a fact that may also explain why he is represented by only eighteen poems in the imperial anthologies.[4] His personal anthology shows him to be more comfortable in the less formal, more personal styles of the courtly recluse.

NOTES

1. For a complete translation, see Keene 1967.
2. See introduction to Tonna, note 1.
3. *Kinrai fūtei, NKT* 5:141.
4. Araki 1977:120-125

Poems

SSZS 2106 (MISCELLANEOUS) Written when he had retired from the world

1
Live here for awhile
   and you're back in the cruel world.
I wish it could be
   as imagined from afar—
my home in the hills.

SZKKS 650 (MISCELLANEOUS) "Cold in the Grass"

2
Arm for my pillow,
I lie on dead leaves of grass
   withered by frost,
my body accustomed now
   to the cold of the wind.[1]

KHS 20 After arranging for a grave site for himself near Side by Side Hills,* he had a cherry tree planted next to it

3
I have made a pledge
to stay beside the blossoms
at Side by Side Hills.
For how many ages to come
will we spend springs together?

* *Narabi no oka,* located just to the south of Ninnaji Temple, in the western outskirts of the capital at Kyōto.

KHS 54 Written when he was in seclusion at Shūgaku-In*

4
There is no place
outside of the cruel world
to hide oneself away,
but escape can still be found
within one's own heart.[2]

* A temple located in the northeastern hills of the capital at Kyōto, on the site of the modern Shūgaku Detached Palace.

KHS 60 "Wild Geese Departing* at Early Dusk"

5
Should you find no inn
    at the end of your cloud-path
        as day nears its end,
    then come back to the capital—
you wild geese of spring!

* The departure of wild geese for the continent was one of the few melancholy events announcing the arrival of spring.

KHS 73 Written in the East Country,* when he found that Mount Fuji†
was in full view from the place where he was staying

6
In the capital
    I used to give my mind
        to thoughts of Fuji—
    now from the hill at my eaves
I can see it anytime.

* Azuma. A term referring in a general way to the provinces east of Kyōto, here more specifically to the area around Kamakura.
† The most famous of Japan's many peaks, located on the border between Kai and Suruga (modern Shizuoka and Yamanashi Prefectures). Poetic convention allowed for smoke rising from the mountain, although there is no evidence that the volcano was active during the late medieval age.

KHS 74 On gulls at play, written on an evening when the face of the sea was utterly calm

7
Off the beach at dusk
   not a wave is to be seen—
the only sight
   is the rise and fall of gulls
     far out over the sea.

KHS 113 "Departing Geese"

8
You departing geese,
why not stop and rest awhile?
On the mountain ridge
   even the clouds hesitate
     as dawn lights the morning sky.

KHS 161 When he was by himself beneath cherry trees

9
Not for the moment
   it would take to tell others
that they've bloomed
   would I want to leave my place
beneath the cherry trees.

10

On Naniwa Strand†
   the tide is at the full
     as a wind comes up;
the reeds‡ are gently swaying,
the plovers are crying.

* *Chidori*. Small shore birds whose plaintive cry is often employed by poets as a symbol of winter loneliness.
† A coastal area in ancient Settsu (modern Ōsaka).
‡ *Ashi*. Common reeds found along ditches, inlets, swamps, etc.

KHS 230 Written when he awoke from a poignant dream and had no one to tell about it

11

I awake from sleep,
but with no one near to tell
   of the dawn dream
that has left my sleeves
   still damp with its tears.

KHS 254 Written when he was walking in the Western Hills,* viewing the cherry blossoms

> 12
> A person I meet
>   invites me to come along
> and so I return
>   along the same mountain road
> to see the blossoms again.

* Nishiyama. On the western border of the capital at Kyōto.

KHS 271 On "Reminiscing in the Rain," from a poem contest in the spring of the fifth year of the Kemmu era [1338]

> 13
> If one is not used
>   to the sound of falling rain
>   around one's grass hut,
> then how can one lose himself
>   in thoughts of the past?[3]

KHS 279 "A Secret Affair Comes to Its End"

> 14
> "O what will I do
>   if the world should find us out?"
> —I used to worry.
> So relief is all I feel
>   as the affair comes to its end.

NOTES

1. An allusive variation on SIS 901, an anonymous Love poem [Headnote: Topic unknown]: "Arm for my pillow, / I used to be chilled by it / as it blew through cracks—/ this wind that my body / has grown accustomed to in time." (*Tamakura no / sukima no kaze mo / samukariki / mi wa narawashi no / mono ni zo arikeru.*)

2. An allusive variation on SZS 1151, by Fujiwara no Shunzei [Headnote: Written on the topic "Deer," when he was composing poems for a hundred-poem sequence of laments]: "From this world of ours / there is simply no escape: even in the hills / where I go to flee my cares / I hear the call of a stag." (*Yo no naka yo / michi koso nakere / omoiiru / yama no oku ni mo / shika zo naku naru.*)

3. An allusive variation on a poem by Bo Juyi (see note 3 in the section on Fujiwara no Teika in this anthology) and to SKKS 201, by Fujiwara no Shunzei [Headnote: A poem on the topic "Cuckoo," written for a hundred-poem sequence requested by the Lay Monk and Former Regent when he was Minister of the Right]: "Musing on the past, / I sit in my hut of grass / amid night showers. / Must you add my tears to the rain, / you cuckoo of the mountain?" (*Mukashi omou / kusa no io no / yoru no ame ni / namida na soe so / yama hototogisu.*)

JAPANESE TEXTS

1 Sumeba mata / ukiyo narikeri / yosonagara / omoishi mama no / yamazato mogana

2 Tamakura no / nobe no kusaba no / shimogare ni / mi wa narawashi no / kaze zo samukeki

3 Chigirioku / hana to narabi no / oka no be ni / aware iku yo no / haru o sugusamu

4 Mi o kakusu / ukiyo no hoka wa / nakeredomo / nogareshi mono wa / kokoro narikeri

5 Yukikururu / kumoji no sue ni / yado nakuba / miyako ni kaere / haru no karigane

6 Miyako nite / omoiyarareshi / fuji no ne o / nokiba no oka ni / idete miru kana

7 Yūnagi wa / nami koso miene / harubaru to / oki no kamome no / tachii nomi shite

8 Kaeru kari / shibashi yasurae / yama no ha no / kumo dani mayou / akebono no sora

9 Minu hito ni / sakinu to tsugemu / hodo dani mo / tachisarigataki / hana no kage kana
10 Naniwagata / michikuru shio ni / kaze tachite / ashi no ha sayagi / chidori naku nari
11 Samenuredo / kataru tomo naki / akatsuki no / yume no namida ni / sode wa nuretsutsu
12 Au hito ni / mata sasowarete / tachikaeri / onaji yamaji no / hana o miru kana
13 Kikinarenu / kusa no iori no / ame no oto ni / mukashi o ikade / omoiizuramu
14 Yo ni moraba / ika ni semu to zo / omoikoshi / kokoro yasuku mo / taeshi naka kana

Jōben (b. 1256?)

Eldest of those disciples of Nijō Tameyo designated the Four Deva Kings of Poetry,[1] Jōben is also the one we know least about. Records make it clear that he was a Tendai priest who attained the rather high ecclesiastical rank of *Hōin* (Dharma Sign); beyond that, however, we know only that he was active in Nijō circles from the mid-1320s to around 1344. An anecdote recorded by the poet Shinkei nearly a century later claiming that Jōben had composed 300,000 poems before the age of fifty must be judged a gross exaggeration, especially when we remember that his extant poems number fewer than a hundred.[2] During his last years—and the headnote to one of his poems indicates that he lived to over eighty—he seems to have lived outside the capital.[3]

Jōben's style, at least insofar as it can be characterized by the few poems he left behind, relies heavily on overtones for its effect and is informed by the medieval aesthetic of *sabi yūgen,* a combination of courtly charm and monochromatic beauty. Although identified with the Nijō faction according to official genealogies, he also seems to have been affected by the "objective" style of Tamekane and his group, like so many other poets of his day.

NOTES

1. See introduction to Tonna, note 1.
2. Ishida 1943:251. For Shinkei's statement, see *Oi no kurigoto, NST* 23:416.
3. Ibid.

Poems

SSZS 1901 (MISCELLANEOUS) On "Bamboo," written for a hundred-poem sequence requested by the Lay Priest Prince Son'en

1

If not for the bamboos
   growing up ever higher
      around your garden,
where else would I find shadows
   to hide myself away?

FGS 1598 (MISCELLANEOUS) "Cold Reeds Around an Inlet"

2

Around the inlet,
standing up out of the ice—
are rows of reeds,*
their frosty leaves rustling
   in the breeze from off the bay.

* *Ashi.* Common reeds found along ditches, inlets, swamps, etc.

3
Did it perhaps
    pledge to stay this night with me
        despite my sad state?
The moonlight on my sleeves
    shows no aversion to my tears.

JS 27 "Early Autumn"

4
What is the reason
    for these feelings of sadness
        rising in my heart?
Since long ago I have known
    the sound of autumn's first wind.

5
A shower* passes by—
and the rays of the evening sun
   make the crimson leaves
of Ogura Mountain†
   shine with a brighter glow.[1]

* Dew, showers, and frost were deemed responsible for leaves changing color in autumn.
† One of the peaks of Tatsuta, a mountainous area just southwest of the old capital at Nara that was noted for its autumn leaves and, to a lesser extent, for its cherry blossoms.

REW (MISCELLANEOUS) From a ten-poem sequence on blossoms requested by Former Major Counselor Tameyo

6
Cherries are blooming
   on Kagu's Heavenly Hill×—
or might it be
   that someone's left a brocade robe
      to dry in the rising sun?

* Ama no Kaguyama. A mountain in central Yamato, south of the old capital at Nara.

NOTES

1. An allusive variation on SIS 215, by Ki no Tsurayuki [Headnote: Written for a standing screen presented at a celebration for Naishi no

Kami during the Engi era]: "Clouds are darkening / the skies with rain showers / on the foot-wearying hills, / but still the crimson leaves / shine with a brighter glow." (*Ashihiki no / yama kakikumori / shigururedo / momiji wa itodo / terimasarikeri.*)

JAPANESE TEXTS

1 Sakaeyuku / take no sonō no / nakariseba / ika naru kage ni / mi o kakusamashi

2 Minatoe no / kōri ni tateru / ashi no ha ni / yūshimo sayagi / urakaze zo fuku

3 Ukimi ni mo / chigirite arite ya / yadoruran / namida itowanu / sode no tsukikage

4 Nani yue ni / sanomi aware no / masaruran / mukashi mo kikishi / aki no hatsukaze

5 Shigurureba / yūhi no kage wa / ogura yama / momiji zo itodo / terimasarikeru

6 Sakura saku / ama no kaguyama / izuru hi ni / ta ga koromode no / nishiki hosu ramu

Nijō Tamesada (1293–1360)

Even though he lost his father at the age of eight, the younger years of Nijō Tamesada, a grandson of Tameyo, were full of promise. Raised by his uncle, who taught him the Nijō style, he assisted in the compilation of the *Shoku goshūishū* (Later Collection of Gleanings Continued, 1325) at a young age, becoming chief compiler of that work upon his uncle's death in 1324. This early success was partly due to his talent, but his sister's marriage to Emperor Go-Daigo (1288–1339) also gave him the most important of allies at court.

Ironically, his relationship with Go-Daigo almost led to Tamesada's undoing as well. For the emperor, already a mature man of thirty when he ascended the throne in 1318, proved to be one of the most headstrong of Japanese sovereigns, a man who made it clear from the beginning that he would not be satisfied with the exercise of ceremonial powers only. His plots against the military government in Kamakura were of course uncovered by spies, and some of the conspirators were punished. But still Go-Daigo continued his intrigues, eventually causing a civil war that would usher in the period of Japanese history known as the Era of the Northern and Southern Courts— the latter being ruled over by the fugitive emperor himself, sequestered deep in the hills of Yoshino.

When forced to choose between the two courts, Tamesada opted for safety over the demands of loyalty. During the first disturbance—the so-called Genkō Uprising of 1331—he secluded himself in a temple in the Eastern Hills of the capital;

and a few years later, when civil war broke out, he likewise attempted to distance himself from the combatants. For a number of years thereafter, however, he was viewed with suspicion by the authorities of the new Ashikaga government, who perhaps knew of his secret contact with friends in the Southern Court.

Meanwhile, other Nijō poets, Tonna especially, were gaining the support of the new shōgun, Ashikaga Takauji. Before long Tamesada was acting as a regular participant in elite poetry gatherings again. After a brief hiatus in which the Kyōgoku-Reizei poets reasserted themselves under the support of Retired Emperors Hanazono and Kōgon, the Nijō style once more held sway in the capital. Thus when a command for a new imperial anthology came in 1356, it came, predictably, to Tamesada, despite his having taken the tonsure as a lay priest several years before. The work, titled the *Shin senzaishū* (New Collection of a Thousand Years), was completed in 1360.

In most ways a rather conventional poet, his style is summed up nicely by Nijō Yoshimoto as "refined" (*kedakashi*) and "lofty and mellifluous" (*yuruyuru to take arite*; see *Kinrai fūtei, NKT* 5:141).

Poems

SHOKUGSIS 57 (SPRING) On "Departing Geese,"* written when some
of the higher ranking courtiers presented ten-verse sequences

> 1
> The Sao Princess†
> > borrows a new robe of haze
> > each and every year:
> is it because they resent her
> > that the wild geese fly away?

* Each spring wild geese depart to summer in Siberia.
† The Goddess of Spring, who made her abode on Sao Mountain to
the east of the old capital at Nara—the direction of spring in Chinese
thought.

From a hundred-poem sequence of the Bumpō era [1317–1319]

2

Spring having passed,
I must make the change today
    into broad-sleeved robes*
that feel strange against my skin—
as strange as summer itself.

* *Karakoromo.* Literally, Chinese robes; here, meaning simply robes of fine, thin fabric worn in summer.

From a hundred-poem sequence composed in the second year of the Jōwa era [1346]

3

The smoke rising
    from the peak of Mount Fuji*
        wanders through the sky—
as uncertain as the thoughts
of my restless heart.[1]

* The most famous of Japan's many peaks, located on the border between Kai and Suruga (modern Shizuoka and Yamanashi Prefectures). Poetic convention allowed for smoke rising from the mountain, although there is no evidence that the volcano was active in the late medieval age.

Presented as part of a hundred-poem sequence, on "Love, with Clouds as an Image"

4

Those high floating clouds
    blown about on the harsh winds
of a winter storm
    have a better chance of meeting
than do I and the one I love.

SSZS 1774 (MISCELLANEOUS) Presented as part of a hundred-poem sequence, on "The Moon"

5

Just biding my time
    night after long autumn night,
I have watched the moon—
with not a thing else to do
    but sit here and grow old.

DT 59 (AUTUMN) "Passing Miscanthus on the Road"

6

Passing travelers
    making their way through this field
        are very few;
yet how tirelessly it beckons—
the flowering miscanthus.*[2]

---

* *Hana susuki*. A large plant resembling pampas grass that flowers each autumn in hills and fields.

7
A shower passes
 and my black-pine hut leaks rain;
and then once again,
through that same crack between boards—
I get a glimpse of the moon.

NOTES

1. An echo of SKKS 1615, by Monk Saigyō [Headnote: Written about Mount Fuji, when he was on a religious pilgrimage in the East Country]: "Smoke on the wind / trailing above Mount Fuji / fades into the sky— / as unsure in destination / as my troubled thoughts." (*Kaze ni nabiku / fuji no keburi no / sora ni kiete / yukue mo shiranu / waga kokoro kana.*)
2. An allusive variation on SKKS 350, by Hachijō-In no Shijō (precise dates unknown) [Headnote: From a hundred-poem sequence commissioned by the Regent-Chancellor]: "To every field / the wind passing on its way / is a visitor— / otherwise it waves in vain— / the flowering miscanthus." (*Nobe goto ni / otozurewataru / akikaze o / ada ni mo nabiku / hana susuki kana.*)

JAPANESE TEXTS

1 Saohime no / koromo karigane / haru goto ni / urami yo tote ya / tachikaeruramu
2 Haru sugite / kyō nugikouru / karakoromo / mi ni koso narenu / natsu wa kinikeri
3 Tachinoboru / fuji no keburi no / yukue tomo / kokoro sora naru / mi no omoi kana
4 Fukimayou / arashi no sora no / ukigumo no / yukiau beku mo / naki chigiri kana

5 Itazura ni / aki no yona yona / tsuki mishi mo / nasu koto nakute /
   mi zo oinikeru
6 Tabibito no / nobe no yukiki wa / shigekarade / hima naku maneku
   / hana susuki kana
7 Murashigure / morite suginuru / maki no ya no / onaji itama ni / tsuki
   o miru kana

Keiun (fl. 1340–1369)

The son and heir of Jōben, Keiun was also a Nijō adherent, youngest of the Four Deva Kings.[1] In early life he seems to have studied on Mt. Hiei; later on he is known to have served in various minor ecclesiastical posts, finally earning the rank of Hōin and title of Provisional Bishop (Gon-Sōzu). But, again like his father, his reputation came to depend on his literary talents. After studying under Tameyo, he went on to study under Tamesada, from whom he received the prized *denju* (house secrets) of the Nijō line, possession of which constituted a stamp of legitimacy for medieval poets of all persuasions. In later years he also received the teachings of the Reizei line from Tamehide.

Nijō Yoshimoto is rather harsh in his appraisal of Keiun's work, saying that he inclined toward "ancient styles" (*chito kotai ni kakarite*), and that he allowed himself too much freedom in both form and theme, as a result producing poems that "grated on the ear" (*mimi ni tatsu sama*).[2] To put it more bluntly, he seems to have been influenced by the Kyōgoku-Reizei ideals of direct expression and deliberate archaism. At the same time, however, Yoshimoto admits that Tamesada had nothing but praise for Keiun.[3] In the end, Keiun emerges from what records we have of his work as an ambiguous figure, a member of the conservative camp, but one who showed occasional impatience with traditional forms and conventions.

If later stories about him can be trusted, it may have been his competitive spirit as much as his poetic style that put Keiun in a difficult position among his Nijō peers. In his *Sasamegoto*

(Whisperings, 1469) the poet-priest Shinkei records that Keiun asked not to have any of his poems included in the *Shin senzaishū* (1359) after he learned that his rival Tonna was going to be more amply represented. (His request seems to have been granted; none of his poems are found in the anthology.) Another anecdote claims that just before death Keuin destroyed all of his poetry out of spite against those who had not appreciated him in his own time. All in all, Shinkei's portrayal of him as an unhappy man who wrote nothing but laments may be close to the truth.[4]

NOTES

1. See introduction to Tonna, note 1.
2. *Kinrai fūtei, NKT* 5:141.
3. Ibid.
4. *Sasamegoto, NKBT* 66.196, 197.

Poems

SGSIS 641 (MISCELLANEOUS-SPRING) Written on the topic "Lark"

1
From my little hut
   high up on the mountain peak
the dusk-lark's voice
   rising from down below
sounds like it's falling away.[1]

SZKKS 1380 (LOVE) On "Intense Passion"

2
Even in my dreams
   I have failed to meet you here,
but in the next world
   —wide awake in the darkness*—
I shall yearn for you still.[2]

* *Yami no utsutsu*. Literally, "reality's darkness." Here, used ironically to refer to the darkness that awaits those in the next world who are still bound by the shackles of love.

3

Far in those heavens
  high up above the clouds,
the haze is spreading—
as smoke rises from Fuji*
  in the faint light of spring dawn.[3]

* The most famous of Japan's many volcanic peaks, located on the border between Kai and Suruga (modern Shizuoka and Yamanashi Prefectures). Poetic convention allowed for smoke rising from the mountain, although there is no evidence that the volcano was active during the late medieval age.

KUHS 48 (SPRING) On "Remaining Blossoms"

4

At this late date
  who will come to visit them?
Far back in these hills,
even the wind seems unaware
  of the remaining blossoms.

5

The wretched hovel
   of some lowly commoner:
even such a place
   has its moment of glory
      when evening faces* blossom.[4]

* *Yūgao no hana*. The moonflower, a kind of gourd with white flowers
that bloom in late summer.

KUHS 91 (AUTUMN) "Early Autumn"

6

I knew it was coming—
and yet the melancholy
   I had prepared for
still strikes me to the quick
   when I hear the autumn wind.

KUHS 168 (WINTER)

7

When grasses and trees
   are completely covered up
      by a snowfall:
that is when the mountains
   appear most open and alone.

8

On the hunting field,
an exhausted game bird
    hides in the high grass;
then to hide him all the more—
the sky darkens into night.[5]

NOTES

1. An allusive variation on SS 120, by Tonna. See poem 6 in the section on Tonna in this anthology.

2. An allusive variation on KKS 647, anonymous [Headnote: Topic unknown]: "But little better / than the vivid dream I dreamt / was our encounter / in reality's darkness, / black as leopard flower seeds." (*Nubatama no / yami no utsutsu wa / sadaka naru / yume ni ikura mo / masarazarikeri.*) McCullough 1985:144.

3. An allusive variation on SKKS 33, by Archbishop Jien [Headnote: Presented as part of a hundred-poem sequence]: "On Heaven's Plain / smoke is rising from Fuji / into the haze / that trails its spring color / through the faint sky of dawn." (*Ama no hara / fuji no keburi no / haru no iro no / kasumi ni nabiku / akebono no sora.*)

4. An allusive variation involving the "Evening Faces" chapter of *The Tale of Genji*, in which Genji has a brief affair with a woman named The Lady of the Evening Faces after the *yūgao* growing around her run-down house (see Seidensticker 1976, 1:57–83), and KKS 888, anonymous [Headnote: Topic unknown]: "The humble man, too, / like the man of high estate, / once enjoyed a prime / when he was brisk as a reel / wound for the striped cloth of old." (*Inishie no / shizu no odamaki / iyashiki mo / yoki mo sakari wa / arishi mono nari.*) McCullough 1985:195.

5. An allusive variation on SKKS 687, by Ōe no Masafusa (d. 1111) [Headnote: Written for a poem contest at the Kayanoin, residence of the Kyōgoku Regent–Former Chancellor]: "On the hunting field / a storm has left everything / buried in snow: / the bird-stand obscured, / hidden in the high grass." (*Mikarino wa / katsu furu yuki ni / uzumorete / todachi*

mo miezu / kusagakuretsutsu). The "bird-stand" is a field prepared near swamps, ponds, and so forth to attract game birds.

JAPANESE TEXTS

1 Io musubu / yama no susono no / yūhibari / agaru mo otsuru / koe ka to zo kiku
2 Yume ni dani / aiminu naka o / nochi no yo no / yami no utsutsu ni / mata ya shitawan
3 Hisakata no / kumoi ni takaku / kasumu nari / fuji no keburi no / haru no akebono
4 Imasara ni / tare ka wa towamu / yama fukami / kaze dani shirade / nokoru sakura o
5 Kaku bakari / shizu ga fuseya no / iyashiki mo / sakari wa miyuru / yūgao no hana
6 Kyō to ieba / kanete omoishi / sabishisa o / nao mi ni shime to / akikaze zo fuku
7 Kusa mo ki mo / uzumorehatsuru / yuki ni koso / naka naka yama wa / arawa narikere
8 Mikarino no / tsukare no tori no / kusagakure / kakurehateyo to / kururu sora kana

Emperor Hanazono (1297–1348)

Born the third son of Emperor Fushimi, the future Emperor Hanazono was taught poetry by two stalwarts of the Kyōgoku cause—his own father and Empress Eifuku. It was during Hanazono's reign, which lasted from 1308 until 1318, that the *Gyoku-yōshū* was commissioned and completed; and after the death of his father in 1317, Hanazono was one of those who did the most to keep the liberal tradition alive.

Although his time, which encompassed the earliest years of the divided courts, was one of trouble and confusion, the emperor was by nature a scholarly sort who kept aloof from political affairs, except insofar as they involved poetry. Thus even during the days of the civil war he was able to spend most of his days in elegant retirement, surrounded by imperial princes and princesses, courtier-poets, and ecclesiastics who shared his interest in the arts. Before going off into exile, Tamekane turned most of his library over to Hanazono; thereafter the retired emperor, using the Zen temple Myōshinji as his detached palace, made use of that gift to dedicate most of his time to scholarship and poetry.

Predictably, Emperor Hanazono had little use for Nijō Tameyo and his cohorts, while for Tamekane and other proponents of the free style he had nothing but praise. Gathering around him the latter's heir, Tamemoto (precise dates unknown), Reizei Tamehide, Ōgimachi Kinkage (1297–1360), and a host of other devotees, he brought about one final florescence of the Kyōgoku-Reizei style. Owing partly to the political confusion of the time, which had left the Nijō branch of the family split into various factions allied with the warring courts, he was able for a time to dominate poetic affairs in the capital.

In 1344 the retired sovereign commissioned an imperial collection to commemorate his efforts. Titled the Collection of Elegance (*Fūgashū*), it was completed several years later, with Emperor Kōgon acting as chief compiler under Emperor Hanazono's direction; the latter himself wrote the work's Chinese and Japanese prefaces. Only once before, at the time of Emperor Go-Toba, had an emperor taken such direct control over the compilation of a collection. The result was a work that most modern critics see as the last of the great imperial collections.

Emperor Hanazono's own poems show the influence of Tamekane in the expected ways—a liberal approach to subject and theme, an occasional impatience with traditional diction, and unusual syntactic patterns. In all, however, his poetry is more melancholy and brooding than the works of Tamekane and his father, who had of course lived in a brighter time. Another important dimension of Hanazono's work is its Buddhist connotations. A student of Zen, in particular, he is counted among the finest religious poets of the court tradition.

Poems

FGS 250 (SPRING) From a hundred-poem sequence

1

Down from the branches
    fall blossoms of the cherry
        in tranquility;
sounding heavy through the haze
    is the voice of the vespers bell.*

* *Iriai no kane.* Rung at temples each evening at around 6 P.M.

FGS 413 (SUMMER) From a hundred-poem sequence

2

Cutting past the front
    of a summer evening shower
        flies a white heron;
on its wings—light from the sun
    still shining where the sky is clear.[1]

FGS 421 (SUMMER) From a hundred-poem sequence

3

Beneath a clear sky,
thick branches almost obscure
    the moonlit night;
a cicada* cries out once,
awakened by the wind.

* *Semi*. A large beetle-like insect whose shrill drone is one of the chief
sounds of the Japanese summer.

FGS 539 (AUTUMN) From a hundred-poem sequence

4

Off in the far clouds
    where the sun has just gone down
        behind a mountain ridge,
they seem not to move at all—
one line of wild geese.*

* In autumn, wild geese return from Siberia to winter in Japan.

5

In the darkening
  of flowering miscanthus*
    waving in the wind,
the moon moves into the distance
  in my garden at dawn.

* *Obana.* Another name for *hana susuki,* flowering miscanthus, a large plant resembling pampas grass that flowers each autumn in hills and fields.

FGS 687 (AUTUMN) On "Autumn Hills," written when he had requested thirty-poem sequences from some of his people

6

The mist clears away
  and at the paddies' far edge
    the hills appear—
rows of rice plants giving way
  to tree upon tree of red leaves.

FGS 878 (WINTER) On the feeling of winter dusk

7

As day fades away
   there is light in the garden—
but only from the snow;
inside it is darker still,
next to my small coal fire.*[2]

* *Uzumibi.* A small banked fire set amid hot coals in a brazier.

FGS 912 (TRAVEL) "On the Road at Dusk"

8

Spreading clouds of mist
   darken the end of my path
     on through the valley,
but still in the evening light
   is the bridge up near the peak.*[3]

* *Kakehashi.* A rope bridge spanning a mountain gorge.

FGS 1064 (LOVE) "Love in the Night"

9

The hour has grown late.
Facing yet another night
   with no visitor,
I gaze at the torchlight's glow,
made brighter by my tears.[4]

Sent to the Retired Emperor along with a sprig of cherry in the spring of the second year of the Ryakuō era [1339]*

10
Unaware of the times,
the cherry tree at my eaves
    is in full bloom.
Won't you please make a visit—
for if not, who else will come?
        —The Retired Empress,
            Eifuku-Mon'in

* When the country was embroiled in the conflicts that began the military rule of the Ashikaga shoguns.

The Retired Emperor's reply:

11
So far from springlike
    is the view from my home
far back in the hills
    that I had quite forgotten
it was time to see blossoms.

FGS 1634 (MISCELLANEOUS) From a hundred-poem sequence

12
With a sound of wings,
a crow passes by above me,
    crying out just once—
with the sky over my eaves
    now entirely clear of clouds.

13

In every household
   busy sounds hurry along
      the break of day—
but how serene is the whitening
   of the sky above the hills.

14

Nothing is left now
   of the tumbledown hovels
      but a bamboo fence—
except for a dog barking
   from way out in the back.[5]

FGS 2056 (BUDDHISM) Written after a statement from the Healing King chapter of *The Lotus Sutra*: "Truly this is an exquisite offering, this is what one calls a true Dharma Offering to the Thus-Come-One."*

15

The sparrows twitter
    near eaves where the evening sun
      is fading away;
the spring wind in the garden
    is green with bending willows.

* Words spoken by the gathered buddhas after the Healing King has burned himself as an offering to the Buddha. The focal point of the poem is the setting sun, a symbol of the Healing King's physical body, whose destruction allows the superior beauty of his buddha-spirit—the wind bending the willows—to appear.[6]

FGS 2073 (BUDDHISM) On an imperial pilgrimage to Chōfukuji, the Emperor expounded the excellence of this *kōan** from *The Blue Cliff Record*: "A monk asked Ummon, 'A tree withers and its leaves fall away—what are we to make of it?' Ummon said, 'The trunk appears in gold wind.'" Then he composed this poem.

16

Tatsuta River
    carries its red autumn leaves
      into fair Yoshino,
the mountains of Yoshino
    where the cherries are in bloom.†

* An anecdote or statement used as a focus in Zen meditation.
† Just as the kōan replies to a question involving autumn imagery with the spring image of "gold wind" (soft wind laden with dew: the "life" of spring versus the "death" of autumn), the poem presents the autumn imagery of Tatsuta together with the spring imagery of Yoshino—the two coming together in one eternal round.

17

How can one hope
   to raise the wick of the light
      that shines on our world?
—when the Lamp of the Law*
   could go out at any moment.

* *Nori no tomoshibi.* The Buddhist Law, compared to a lamp that guides
in the darkness of human folly. Since the end of the Heian period (784–
1185), the devout had believed that their time was the age of the End
of the Law (*mappō* or *masse*), a degenerate period of wickedness that
would last for ten thousand years. Here Hanazono treats the idea im-
agistically, probably thinking of the constant strife of his age as a con-
firmation of the masse doctrine.

RAKUSHO ROKEN 28, in *SKKT* 5

18

I arise and see
   my eaves in the morning light,
shining white with frost;
the wind, making not a sound,
strikes my body with a chill.

NOTES

1. An allusive variation on GYS 416, by Fujiwara no Teika [Head-
note: Topic unknown]: "From the clouds / of a summer evening
shower / sunlight breaks through; / across this side of the mountain /
flies a white heron." (*Yūdachi no / kumoma no hikage / haresomete / yama
no konata o / wataru shirasagi.*)

2. An echo of a poem by Emperor Fushimi: "Blinds separate me / from the snow in my garden / as in my bedchamber / I sit far back in darkness / next to my small coal fire." (*Niwa no yuki wa / sudare hedatsuru / neya no uchi ni / mata oku fukaki / uzumibi no moto.*) Quoted in *Fūgashū*, Iwasa and Tsugita, eds., p. 192.

3. An echo of SKKS 953, by Fujiwara no Teika. See poem 21 in the section on Fujiwara no Teika in this anthology.

4. An echo of a poem by Empress Eifuku. See poem 20 in the section on Empress Eifuku in this anthology.

5. An allusive variation on GYS 2257, by Fujiwara no Teika. See poem 35 in the section on Fujiwara no Teika in this anthology.

6. For a more complete description of the poem's allegorical significance, see Brower and Miner 1961:367–368.

JAPANESE TEXTS

1 Kozue yori / ochikuru hana mo / nodoka nite / kasumi ni omoki / iriai no koe

2 Yūdachi no / kumo tobiwakaru / shirasagi no / tsubasa ni kakete / haruru hi no kage

3 Sora harete / kozue iro koki / tsuki no yo no / kaze ni odoroku / semi no hitokoe

4 Kumo tōki / irihi no ato no / yamagiwa ni / iku to mo mienu / kari no hitotsura

5 Kaze ni nabiku / obana ga sue ni / kageroite / tsuki tōku naru / ariake no niwa

6 Kiri haruru / tatsura no sue ni / yama miete / inaba ni tsuzuku / kiki no momijiba

7 Kureyaranu / niwa no hikari wa / yuki ni shite / oku kuraku naru / uzumibi no moto

8 Kumokiri ni / wakeiru tani wa / suekurete / yūhi nokoreru / mine no kakehashi

9 Fukenikeri / mata towarede to / mukau yo no / namida ni niou / tomoshibi no kage

10 Toki shiranu / yado no nokiba no / hanazakari / kimi dani toe na / mata tare o ka wa

11 Haru utoki / miyamagakure no / nagame yue / tou beki hana no / koro mo wasurete

12 Haoto shite / wataru karasu no / hitokoe ni / nokiba no sora wa / kumo akenu nari

13 Satozato no / akeyuku oto wa / isogedomo / nodoka ni shiramu / yama no ha no sora

14 Ato mo naki / shizugaiei no / take no kaki / inu no koe nomi / oku-fukaku shite

15 Tsubame naku / nokiba no yūhi / kage kiete / yanagi ni aoki / niwa no harukaze

16 Tatsutakawa / momijiba nagaru / miyoshino no / yoshino no yama ni / sakurabana saku

17 Yo o terasu / hikari o ikade / kakagemashi / kenaba kenu beki / nori no tomoshibi

18 Okite miru / asaake no nokiba / shimo shiroshi / oto senu kaze wa / mi ni samuku shite

Emperor Kōgon (1313–1364)

Emperor Kōgon, son of Emperor Go-Fushimi and grandson of Emperor Fushimi, was granted the distinction of serving as the first emperor of the Northern Court—although he reigned for only a short while before his position was usurped by his bellicose cousin Go-Daigo. Thereafter he became the In, or Retired Emperor, devoting his time·to what had become the tradition of his house—poetry.

Kōgon was tutored in the style of the Kyōgoku-Reizei poets by his uncle, Emperor Hanazono, and participated with the latter in the compilation of the *Fūgashū* (1344–1346). Unlike his uncle, however, he lived on to see the traditions of his line die out almost completely, first because of the dominance of the Nijō school under the direction of Tamesada and Tonna, and later because of the political upheavals of the early 1350s, which sent him away from the capital for safety. He took the tonsure in 1352, and although he returned to the capital several years later, he left once again in 1362 to undertake pilgrimages to various temples in the home provinces. He died at a temple in Tamba province in the early autumn of 1364, in surroundings more befitting a lowly Zennist than a retired emperor. Records of his last years show almost no evidence of a continuing interest in poetry (see Iwasa 1976:63–65).

Kōgon is one of the most interesting of the Kyōgoku poets. Like Emperor Hanazono, he was a student of Zen Buddhism. Perhaps for this reason, as well as because of his long sojourns away from the capital, his work seems almost uncourtly at times, having more in common with the linked-verse poets of the next century or with the *haikai* master Bashō than with the conventional poetry of his own day.

Poems

FGS 20 (SPRING) On "Spring Haze"

1
The Plain of Heaven*
    is covered over
with a haze so calm
    that the colors of springtime
remain tightly locked away

* *Ama no hara.* A conventional metaphor for the sky.

FGS 129 (SPRING) From a hundred-poem sequence

2
Shapes of swallows
    appear beyond my reed blinds
        in great numbers;
in the calm of this spring day
    no human shadow passes by.

FGS 266 (SPRING) From a hundred-poem sequence

3
Even the frogs' voices
    calling from out in the water
        seem worn and old;
at a pond surrounded by trees
    spring is approaching its end.

FGS 579 (AUTUMN) From a hundred-poem sequence

4
From a clump of grass
    an insect begins to chirp—
bringing on nightfall;
the surface of the white sand
    is gone to moonlight.[1]

FGS 646 (AUTUMN) From among his Autumn poems

5
Burdened with raindrops,
leaves from the paulownia*
    fall with such a heavy sound
that the downpour seems lighter—
a passing autumn shower.

* *Kiri*. A deciduous tree of the figwort family with large, fan-shaped
yellow leaves that carpet the ground around the trees in autumn.

6

The evening sun shines
   over fallen leaves still wet
      from a passing shower;
in the garden, a confusion
   of shadows from floating clouds.

FGS 880 (WINTER) From among his Winter poems

7

When I stop to think
   of my people lying cold
      in their huts of straw,
I find myself embarassed
   beneath my bedclothes of fine cloth.*[2]

* *Fusuma.* Heavy bedding used by the high-born in winter.

FGS 1629 (MISCELLANEOUS) From among his Miscellaneous poems

8

A crow in the night
   cries once from high in the trees,
then falls down and away;
the moon is peaceful
   over the mountains at dawn.[3]

On the topic "Far and Near," written for a five-verse poem contest

> 9
> Hung low with clouds,
> the pines on those distant hills
>   are not to be seen;
> the bamboo slats in my fence
>   are dripping with rain.

From among his Miscellaneous poems

> 10
> Burning sun and clouds,
> the cold and the heat—
> all have their season.
> And thus the hearts of my people
>   have no time for rest.

"Summer Evening"

> 11
> When I look and see
>   more and more smoke rising
>   from mosquito smudges,*
> I know that day is ending—
> then the sound of the vespers bell.†

* *Kayaribi*. A small scented smudge burned at night to keep away mosquitoes.
† *Iriai no kane*. Rung at temples each evening at around 6 P.M.

12
What was I thinking—
to conclude that autumn nights
    are the most lonely?
Water rails* are calling tonight
    in the light of the moon.

* *Kuina*. Small marsh birds whose deceptive call—referred to as "knocking" in Japanese—leaves its hearer wishing for a knock on the door from a human visitor.

KIS 39 (AUTUMN)

13
The last weak rays
    of the sinking sun
        vanish from my wall;
out in the garden, the chill
    of autumn wind at dusk.

KIS 53 (WINTER)

14
The moon at evening
    in a sky of high branches
        and frozen clouds—
burnished by storm winds,
even its rays seem cold.

KIS 76 (WINTER) "Night Snow"

15
White is the thin snow
    on the roof above the eaves;
clear after a storm,
the sky is full of stars
    gleaming with pure light.

KIS 124 (LOVE) A Love poem

16
That widowed crow
    cawing away at the moon
        is just like me:
all alone, I cannot sleep,
longing for my lost mate.

KIS 141 (MISCELLANEOUS) From among his Miscellaneous poems

17
As the night grows late,
the lamp before my window
    is burning low—
its light now at peace,
as I too am at peace.

18

For a hundred years
the butterfly disports itself
among the flowers,
but shorter by far is its time
awake in the world of men.*

* A vague allusion to Zhuang Zi's famous story of a man who dreamt
he was a butterfly, and then woke up wondering whether he was a but-
terfly dreaming he was a man, or vice-versa.

NOTES

1. A possible allusive variation on GYS 196, by Empress Eifuku. See
poem 1 in the section on Empress Eifuku in this anthology.
2. An allusive variation on ShokuGSS 1093, by Retired Emperor
Go-Toba [Headnote: Topic unknown]: "So cold is the night / that even
through my fine bedclothes / I feel chilled—/ making me think of the
wind / blowing through huts of straw." (*Yo o samumi / neya no fusuma
no / sayuru ni mo / wuraya no kaze o / omoi koso yare.*)
3. An allusive variation on MYS 1263, anonymous: "The day is
breaking, / the night-crow seems to cry—/ but in the treetops / up on
this mountain height / everything is still." (*Akatoki to / yokarasu nakedo
/ kono oka no / konure no ue wa / imada shizukeshi.*)

JAPANESE TEXTS

1 Ama no hara / ōu kasumi no / nodokeki ni / haru naru iro no / ko-
   moru narikeri
2 Tsubakurame / sudare no soto ni / amata miete / haruhi nodokemi
   / hitokage mo sezu
3 Minosoko no / kawazu no koe mo / mono furite / kobukaki ike
   no / haru no kuregata

4   Kusamura no / mushi no koe yori / kuresomete / masago no ue zo / tsuki ni narinuru

5   Nurete otsuru / kiri no kareba wa / oto omomi / arashi wa karoki / aki no murasame

6   Yūhi sasu / ochiba ga ue ni / shigure sugite / niwa ni midaruru / ukigumo no kage

7   Samukarashi / tami no waraya o / omou ni wa / fusuma no naka no / ware mo hazukashi

8   Yogarasu wa / takaki kozue ni / nakiochite / tsuki shizuka naru / akatsuki no yama

9   Kumo kakaru / tōyama matsu wa / miezu narite / magaki no take ni / ame koboru nari

10 Terikumori / samuki atsuki mo / toki toshite / tami ni kokoro no / yasumu ma no nashi

11 Kayaribi no / keburi masaru to / miru hodo ni / kurenuru narashi / iriai no koe

12 Aki no yo o / sabishiki mono to / nani ka omou / kuina koe suru / yoi no tsukikage

13 Shizumu hi no / yowaki hikari wa / kabe ni kiete / niwa susamajiki / aki kaze no kure

14 Kumo kōru / kozue no sora no / yūzukuyo / arashi ni migaku / kage mo samukeshi

15 Noki no ue wa / usuyuki shiroshi / furiharuru / sora ni wa hoshi no / kage kiyoku shite

16 Tsuki ni naku / yamomekarasu wa / waga gotoku / hitorine katami / tsuma ya koishiki

17 Sayo fukuru / mado no tomoshibi / tsukuzuku to / kage mo shizukeshi / ware mo shizukeshi

18 Hana no uchi ni / asobu kochō no / momotose yo / samuru utsutsu wa / nao ya mijikaki

Reizei Tamehide (1302?–1372)

Born the second son of Tamesuke, founder of the Reizei line, Tamehide appears to have spent the first half of his life in the East Country, where he developed a close relationship with the Ashikaga family that was to prove useful to him in later years. Moving to Kyōto in the mid 1340s, he was greeted as an ally in the Kyōgoku cause by Retired Emperors Hanazono and Kōgon, who appointed him as one of the assistant compilers of the *Fūgashū*. At the same time, however, he was one of the regular participants in the poetry gatherings of Nijō Tamesada, who was evidently impressed by his poetic talent.

In the late 1450s Tamehide had a falling out with Tamesada that resulted in his being denied any representation in the *Shin senzaishū* (1359). But after Tamesada's death in 1360, Tamehide remained on close terms with the Nijō heir, Tameakira, even going so far as to place his own oldest son, Tamekuni, in Tameakira's family as a ward. Among other things, this meant that the Reizei family was able to gain access to the teachings of the Nijō line, a fact that Tamehide and his descendents used to his advantage in the internecine squabbles of the time.

From 1360 until his death in 1372, Tamehide was the chief poetic figure of the capital, his only true rivals being Tonna, who of course was in no position to compete on an equal basis with a man of Teika's bloodline who was by that time a Middle Counselor in the court government; and Nijō Yoshimoto, who as a high-ranking courtier was in a different category altogether. Poetic tutor to the shōgun Yoshiakira, Tamehide also counted the regent Nijō Yoshimoto among his supporters. Among his disciples were Imagawa Ryōshun and the linked-verse master Takayama Bontō (d. 1417).

Despite his connections with the Nijō branch of the family, Tamehide was definitely an advocate of Kyōgoku values in his own work, which continues the free, open approach of his father.

Poems

From among his poems on blossoms

> 1
> Blooming everywhere,
> and with no sign of scattering—
> cherries at their height.
> I would not begrudge a breeze
>   if it would blow their scent my way.*

* Poetic convention held that cherry blossoms had a fine scent, although in actuality they have no scent at all.

Topic unknown

> 2
> In the gloom of dusk
>   I can no longer make out
>   the blossoms near my fence.
> But the mists cannot obstruct
>   the voice of a stag.

3

The lightning struck
and even in the brief flash
of its short-lived light
I could count the dewdrops
on the leaves of the grasses.

FGS 619 (AUTUMN) A Moon poem

4

As the mist clears away,
the base of a far-off mountain
comes into clear view;
moonbeams are polishing
the waves in Uji River.*[1]

* A river running through the Uji area, south of capital at Kyōto.

FGS 648 (AUTUMN) Presented as part of hundred-poem sequence

5

I thought it was mist
beginning to rise—
that autumn rain
sprinkling down so softly
in the sky at dusk.

Presented as part of hundred-poem sequence

6

I may well once more
   travel on that self-same path
    within my dreams—
it is the real world now past
   that is so fleeting and vain.

SIS 1241 (LOVE) On "A Changed Lover," written at the house of the Regent and Former Minister of the Left when the poets were "searching for topics"*

7

First you notice
   a change in your lover's words—
that is how you know
   the true complexion
    of the cruel man's heart.

* *Dai o saguru.* An informal poem contest in which poets gathered to compose poems extemporaneously on topics written out, placed on a dais, and then chosen at random.

8
How hard it is
to find a true-hearted friend
in this world of ours!
Alone, I listen all night
to the autumn rain.

NOTE

1. An echo of GYS 2801, by Retired Emperor Go-Toba [Headnote: "Moon Shining on a Coast"]: "On Kiyomi Strand / the smoke from Mount Fuji / must have vanished: / moonbeams are polishing / the waves of Miho Bay." (*Kiyomigata / fuji no keburi / kienuramu / tsukikage migaku / miho no uranami.*)

JAPANESE TEXTS

1 Sakimichite / chirubeku mo aranu / hanazakari / kaoru bakari no / kaze wa itowazu

2 Kureutsuru / magaki no hana wa / miewakade / kiri ni hedatenu / saoshika no koe

3 Inazuma no / shibashi mo tomenu / hikari ni mo / kusaba no tsuyu no / kazu wa miekeri

4 Kiri haruru / ochi no yamamoto / arawarete / tsukikage migaku / uji no kawanami

5 Tachisomuru / kiri ka to mireba / aki no ame no / komaka ni sosogu / yūgure no sora

6 Mata kayou / onaji yumeji mo / aru mono o / arishi utsutsu zo / utate hakanaki

7 Koto no ha no / kawaru ni tsukete / ukibito no / kokoro no iro mo / mazu shiraretsutsu

8 Nasake aru / tomo koso kataki / yo narikeri / hitori ame kiku / aki no yosugara

Nijō Tameshige (1325–1385)

Another of Tameyo's many grandsons, Nijō Tameshige spent his early years as amanuensis to his uncle, Tamesada, from whom he received the "secret teachings" of the family. Because he was born to a lesser wife, however, he was denied the usual titles and privileges of the Nijō heir until late in life. Only after years of study and work did he finally succeed in becoming the *waka* instructor to Ashikaga Yoshimitsu. He also took part in the compilation of the *Shin goshūishū* (New Later Collection of Gleanings, 1383), second to last of the imperial anthologies.

If it can be trusted as authentic, an anecdote recorded by Shōtetsu half a century after Tameshige's death tells us that he was a less than handsome man, but one who had a sense of humor:

> Tameshige was an exceptionally ugly man. One time, in the Palace, he took the hand of a lady he happened to pass and asked if she would spend the night with him. "What?" came her reply, "With a man with such a face!" Then he wrote this poem:

> > That was the reason
> > I asked you to spend the *night*—
> > with the same intent
> > as the ugly god
> > of Katsuragi![1]

Tameshige was occasionally criticized by Tonna and others of the Nijō tradition for his departures from the orthodox style. Yoshimoto, however, describes him as having an inborn talent for the art. Despite his Nijō affiliations, he seems to have been something of a free spirit.[2]

One record indicates that Tameshige was murdered by brigands; another that he was beaten to death by one Lay Priest Hirai, a steward of the Yamashina family. That his son, Tamemigi (d. 1399?), seems to have suffered a similar fate but at a much younger age speaks poignantly for the violence of the times in which both men lived.[3] With Tamemigi's death the Nijō family line came to an end.

NOTES

1. *Shōtetsu monogatari*, NKBT 65:177. The God of Katsuragi was known for his ugliness.
2. *Kinrai fūtei*, NKT 5:141–143.
3. Inoue 1984:31.

Poems

SGSIS 195 (SUMMER) On "Cuckoo* in a Country Village."

1
He must be heading
   across the hills this morning—
that calling cuckoo.
Before long he will be heard
   at Otowa Village.†[1]

---

* *Hototogisu*. A small bird of the cuckoo family whose call was believed
to announce the arrival of summer.
† Located in Yamashina, on the northeast outskirts of the capital at
Kyōto.

2
At Naniwa bay,†
frost freezes on the shore reeds
    night after night;
then, scattering the dead leaves,
comes the wind from off the sea.

* *Ashi*. Common reeds found along ditches, inlets, swamps, etc.
† Naniwae. A coastal area in ancient Settsu (modern Ōsaka) known for
its reeds.

SGSIS 1077 (LOVE) On "A Pledge of Love," from a hundred-poem
sequence

3
If our love too
    is to follow the pattern
        of this world of lies,
then what am I to do
    to make my own promise last?[2]

4

The snow is all gone,
and the ice too has melted.
Far upriver
in the spring fields of Kose,*
they are gathering new greens.†

* Located in southern Yamato (modern Nara Prefecture).
† *Wakana*. Edible herbs and sprouts, the gathering of which was one
of the first activities of spring in the court calendar.

SZKKS 331 (AUTUMN) "Autumn Evening," from a hundred-poem
sequence

5

Only one thing*
can give me understanding
of the pain I feel;
and surely this is not it—
this autumn evening.

* What the "one thing" is remains unclear, but judging from other poems
using the same vocabulary, it may be taking the tonsure as a priest. See
for example SKKS 1753 and 1829.

TAE 14 "Red Leaves"

6

Deep into autumn,
the faint red-colored leaves
    are used to the dew;
now they wait for the showers
    to dye them brighter still.*

* Dew, showers, and frost were deemed responsible for leaves changing color in autumn.

TAE 91 "Winter Moon"

7

Even late at night
    one can see the icy surface
        of the mountain stream;
how cold among the boulders
    is the light of the moon![3]

8

The paddy keeper*
   has dozed off for a moment
      in his hillside hut:
but still pulling at the clapper†
   is the passing autumn wind.

* A man who watches over the paddies at harvest time to keep deer
and other animals from destroying the crop.
† *Hita.* A wooden clapper attached to a rope that the paddy guard pulls
to scare off birds.

TAE 303 From a group of twenty poems composed at the Kuga house
on the fifth day of the month

9

The mountain people
   making their way toward home
      have trampled the leaves—
so that now there is no sound
   in the valley wind at dusk.[4]

NOTES

1. An allusive variation on KKS 142, by Ki no Tomonori (d. before
905?) [Headnote: Hearing a cuckoo as he crossed Otowayama]: "Jour-
neying onward / over Otowayama / while the day is young, / I hear a
cuckoo singing / high in the distant treetops." (*Otowayama / kesa
koekureba / hototogisu / kozue haruka ni / ima zo naku naru.*) McCullough
1985:41.
2. An allusive variation on KKS 712, anonymous [Headnote: Topic

unknown]: "If this were a world / in which there were no such thing / as false promises, / how great would be my delight / as I listened to your words!" (*Itsuwari no / naki yo nariseba / ika bakari / hito no koto no ha / ureshikaramashi.*) McCullough 1985:157.

3. An allusive variation on SKKS 631, by Fujiwara no Shunzei [Headnote: Topic unknown]: "Freezing in one place / breaking up in another, / the mountain stream / is choked between great boulders— / a low moan raised at dawn." (*Katsu kōri / katsu wa kudakuru / yamakawa no / iwama ni musubu / akatsuki no koe.*)

4. An allusive variation on SKKS 558, by Fujiwara no Kiyosuke (1104–1177) [Headnote: Topic unknown]: "All of itself / it makes the only sound / in my garden court / as it blows the leaves about— / the valley wind at dusk." (*Onozukara / oto suru mono wa / niwa no omo ni / konoha fukimaku / tani no yūkaze.*)

JAPANESE TEXTS

1   Yamaji o ba / kesa koenu to ya / hototogisu / yagate otowa no / sato ni nakuran
2   Naniwae ya / ashi no yona yona / shimo kōri / kareba midarete / ura-kaze zo fuku
3   Itsuwari no / aru yo ni narau / naka naraba / waga kanegoto mo / ikaga nokosan
4   Yuki mo kie / kōri mo tokete / kawakami no / kose no haruno wa / wakana tsumu nari
5   Hitokata ni / omoiwaku beki / mi no usa no / sore ni mo aranu / aki no yūgure
6   Aki fukami / tsuyu ni wa nareshi / usumomiji / somuru shigure no / hodo ya matsuran
7   Yamakawa no / kōri no ue mo / yoru miete / iwama ni samuki / tsuki no kage kana
8   Moru hito mo / shibashi madoromu / oyamada ni / hita hiku bakari / akikaze zo fuku
9   Yamabito no / kaesa no konoha / fumiwakete / soyogu to mo naki / tani no yūkaze

Nijō Yoshimoto (1320–1388)

Heir to one of the Five Houses of the Regency (Go-Sekke), Nijō Yoshimoto—a man in no way related to the Nijō poetic family, despite the similarity in names—was one of the most important scholar-bureaucrats of his century. Appointed regent four times, under four different emperors, he was a scholar of court lore and literature, a poet in all the major genres of the court tradition, an important critic and literary historian, a connoisseur of the arts of calligraphy and perfume blending, and a fine stylist in prose genres such as the travel diary.

It is as a theorist and codifier of linked verse *(renga)* that Yoshimoto is most remembered now. And, indeed, it was to linked verse that he dedicated much of his literary effort, producing a number of important essays on that genre's history and proper composition, an important rulebook, and the first imperially recognized collection of the form—the *Tsukubashū* (1356). But from his mid-twenties on he was also an important figure in the world of uta as well. His *Kinrai fūtei,* a short treatise-memoir written just a year before his death, shows that he was acquainted with most of the important poets of his time, including Tameyo, Tametada (1309–1373), Tamesada, Tameakira, Tameshige, Tonna, Keiun, and Kenkō on the Nijō side, and Emperors Hanazono and Kōgon, Tamehide, Tamekuni, and Imagawa Ryōshun on the Kyōgoku-Reizei side. His characterizations of these and other poets are now valued highly by critics.[1]

Despite his affection for Emperor Go-Daigo, Yoshimoto stayed with the Northern Court in 1336, becoming increasingly involved in court poetry meetings from that time forward. In *Kinrai fūtei,* he admits to having been taken with the "unorthodox style" *(ifū)* of the Kyōgoku-Reizei poets surrounding Emperor Hanazono in his early years;[2] after 1350, however, he became a convert to the Nijō cause and spent the rest of his life as a conservative figure at court. In particular, he seems to have respected Tonna, with whom he wrote an important treatise on poetics in 1363.[3] Toward the end of his life he was privileged to write the Japanese preface for the *Shin goshūishū;* with the death of Tameshige in 1385, he became the grand old man of Nijō letters, holding poetry contests and acting as a patron to the arts in general.

Yoshimoto was not a great poet in the uta form. But one of the virtues of the conservative approach was that it could make almost any educated person into a passable versifier, as the evidence of his poems makes clear.

NOTES

1. *NKT* 5:141–153.
2. *NKT* 5:143.
3. *Gumon kenchū, NKT* 5:123–140.

Poems

FGS 540 (AUTUMN) From a hundred-poem sequence

> 1
> In the setting sunlight
>   spilling from a break in the clouds,
> one can count them—
> wild geese* passing on their way
>   far off across the sky.

* In autumn, wild geese return from Siberia to winter in Japan.

FGS 584 (AUTUMN) An Autumn poem, from among poems presented as a hundred-poem sequence

> 2
> Now, at long last,
> the moon that kept me waiting
>   is starting to glow;
> clustered clouds are turning white
>   in the sky above the ridge.

Nijō Yoshimoto 241

3

In the light of dawn
    illuminating branches
        white with fallen snow,
there is a faint hint of red—
the year's first plum blossoms.

SGSIS 417 (AUTUMN) Topic unknown

4

As the night deepens,
dewdrops begin to appear
    out back on the fields—
but more numerous by far
    are the insect voices.

SGSIS 575 (WINTER) From *The Hundred-Poem Sequences of the Embun Era* [1356]

5

As the old year ends,
I think less of spring's approach
    than of my old age,
which they say comes on the same path
—at an even faster pace.[1]

6

In the morning mist
  a boat parts the breaking
    waves along the shore,
almost fading from sight
  before it is out to sea.[2]

7

My heart is clear now,
used to the storm winds
  blowing in the pines—
but it's not as if I've fled
  to a hut back in the hills.*

* In other words, he has not turned his back on the world as a monk-recluse.

NOTES

1. An allusive variation on KKS 349, by Ariwara no Narihira [Headnote: Composed when there was a fortieth-year celebration for the Horikawa Chancellor at the Kujō Mansion]: "Scatter at random, / O blossoms of the cherry / and cloud the heavens, / that you may conceal the path / old age is said to follow." (*Sakurabana / chirikaikumore / oiraku no / komu to iu naru / michi magau ga ni.*) McCullough 1985:84.

2. An allusive variation on KKS 409, attributed to Kakinomoto Hitomaro [Headnote: Topic unknown]: "In the dim, dim light / of the early morning mist / on Akashi Bay, / a boat fades behind the isles— /

my heart following in its wake." (*Honobono to / akashi no ura no / asagiri ni / shimagakureyuku / fune o shi zo omou.*)

JAPANESE TEXTS

1 Kumoma moru / irihi no kage ni / kazu miete / tōchi no sora o / wataru karigane
2 Ima shi haya / mataruru tsuki zo / niourashi / murakumo shiroki / yama no ha no sora
3 Furikakaru / kozue no yuki no / asaake ni / kurenai usuki / ume no hatsubana
4 Yoi no ma ni / oku naru nobe no / tsuyu yori mo / nao koto shigeki / mushi no koe kana
5 Ima wa mi ni / kon to iu naru / oiraku no / haru yori chikaki / toshi no kure kana
6 Asagiri ni / iso no nami wake / yuku fune wa / oki ni idenu mo / tōzakaritsutsu
7 Kokoro sumu / matsu no arashi mo / naretekeri / nogaruru yama no / oku naranedomo

Prince Munenaga (b. 1311)

If there is a special poignancy in the poems of Prince Munenaga, it is perhaps due to the unhappy circumstances of his life. Born the son of Emperor Go-Daigo while the latter was still Crown Prince, he had every reason to look forward to a bright career at court as a young man. When his father's political ambitions led to civil war in the 1330s, however, he found himself a permanent refugee forced to live by the sword, leading southern loyalist armies through the more remote regions of the central provinces and beyond.

Before political events took him away from Kyōto, Munenaga seemed destined for the religious life, acting first as the abbot of a prominent monastery and later as Tendai Zasu, chief of the powerful Tendai sect. It was after the Genkō disturbance of 1331, when he was still an ecclesiastic, that he was first sent away from the capital to exile in Sanuki. In 1337 he cast off his monkish robes and became a standard bearer in the Southern army, spending most of the next thirty years in mountainous Shinano, Echigo, and Etchū. In 1374, he returned to Yoshino, but died back in Shinano sometime before 1389.

Particularly close to Nijō Tamesada in his youth, the prince remained a Nijō conservative his entire life, creating his own salon among loyalist friends after participation in the artistic life of the capital became impossible. For political reasons, none of his poems was included in either the *Fūgashū* (1346) or the *Shin senzaishū* (1360).[1] In order to assure himself a place in the history of court poetry, he therefore took it upon himself to compile the only imperially commissioned anthology to originate from the Southern Court, the *Shinyōshū* (Collection of New Leaves), which was completed in 1381 and accorded status as a *jun-chokusenshū* (imperial collection of the second rank) by Emperor Chōkei (1343–1394). Ironically, this work, produced by exiles from the capital, is in many ways the last of the truly courtly imperial collections, including only a handful of poems from the military classes—in obvious contrast to the anthologies produced by the Northern Court, which were sponsored and greatly influenced by the Ashikaga shōguns and their retainers.[2]

In addition to its deeply nostalgic tone, Prince Munenaga's poetry is informed by the aesthetic of *mujō* (impermanence). In diction and form his poems generally reflect the plain elegance of his Nijō friends in the capital, although his long experience in the provinces seems to have given his work a coarser texture than is usually found among the poems of the court aristocracy.

NOTES

1. Several of his poems later appeared anonymously in *Shin zoku-kokinshū* (1439), the last of the imperial anthologies.
2. Kubota et al. 1976:257–258.

Poems

SYS 113 (SPRING) In the spring of the fourth year of the Engen era [1339], the Prince came back from the East Country* to Yoshino,† where he spent a number of days in the temporary palace. This poem came from Former Major Counselor Tamesada:

> 1
> Won't you please hasten
>   your return to your true home?
> —even if those famous
>   mountain cherry blossoms
>   should tug at your heart to say.‡

* Azuma. A term referring in a general way to the provinces east of Kyōto.
† A mountainous area in central Yamato (modern Nara Prefecture), where the Southern loyalists had their court.
‡ In the original anthology Tamesada's poem is quoted in the headnote to the poem by Prince Munenaga that follows.

[Prince Munenaga's reply:]

> 2
> You know how I long
>   to be back in my true home—
> but how could I leave
>   without seeing the full bloom
>   of the blossoms of Yoshino?

SYS 218 (AUTUMN) Sent to a person in the capital when he was living in Shinano*

> **3**
> Take pity on me!
> The road to the capital
>   is blocked by dense clouds
> that drop their endless showers
>   on my side of the mountain.

* A rugged area in the Japan Alps (modern Nagano Prefecture) where the poet was in hiding with forces of the Southern Court.

SYS 247[1] (AUTUMN) On "Autumn's Beginning," from among poems presented as a thousand-poem sequence

> **4**
> The wind is rustling
>   through the yearning-bamboo*
>   on the reedy† meadows:
> now people will realize
>   that the autumn has begun.

* *Shinohara*. A kind of dwarf bamboo. Used here for the punning possibilities of its name—*shino* meaning "to yearn for."
† *Asaji*. Cogon grass—a short reed-like plant that grows in clumps on moorlands and meadows. In poetry, it carries a melancholy connotation and is generally shown thriving around run-down or abandoned homes.

SYS 497 (WINTER) Presented as part of a thousand-poem sequence

5

Above Ōhara*
    the fallen snow has piled up
        and all paths are gone.
For this one day, no burning, please—
charcoal kiln up on the peak!

* An area on the western outskirts of the capital at Kyōto.

SYS 624[2] (BUDDHISM) Written on the idea of "Individual Enlightenment"*

6

Fallen away now
    are the blossoms and red leaves
        I once gazed upon:
and the color of my heart
    is now blank and empty.[3]

* *Engaku;* Sanskrit *pratyekabuddha.* Literally, a stage of enlightenment arrived at without the aid of a master—a state symbolized in the poem by the emptiness of a heart free of the illusions represented by sensory perception.

SYS 696 (LOVE) Among the poems of a hundred-poem sequence presented at Kitano Shrine*

7
What am I to do?
—the sleeves of my robe
    not being a weir†
set to stem the rapid flow
    of my gushing tears.

* The most prominent of Kyōto shrines during the late medieval period, located on the northwestern border of the city.
† *Shigarami*. A small dam of sticks set in a river current to catch fish.

SYS 734 (LOVE) Among the poems of a hundred-poem sequence composed while he was on the road

8
The pain is greater now—
at least while we were living
    in the same capital
the only thing between us
    was the wall of her hard heart.

SYS 921[4] (LOVE) Written when something was on his mind, during the Godless Month* as he was watching the leaves falling from the trees

9

At this year's end too
   I will be paid a visit—
by autumn's harshness
      blowing through the upper leaves
         of the weeds† around my house.

* *Kannazuki*. The tenth month in the lunar calendar.
† *Yomogiu*. Literally, mugwort, a spreading vine. In poetry, it usually grows around run-down or abandoned homes and is similar in connotation to *asaji* (cogon grass).

SYS 1306 (MISCELLANEOUS) After having gone to the East Country* in the Engen era [1336–1340], he finally came back to the Yoshino Palace* in the winter of the third year of the Bunchū era [1374], only to find no one left there from his own time. While caught up in his memories, he composed this poem on "Remembering the Past Alone"

10

O how I long
   for a friend who has seen
      the same world as I!
—if only so we could share
   our longing for the past.

* Referring to the mountains of Yoshino in central Yamato (modern Nara Prefecture), where the Southern loyalists had their court.

On "Reminiscing in Old Age," presented as part of a thousand-poem sequence

> 11
> In times yet to come
>   will someone tell of my day?
> —of things long ago
>   that before an old man's eyes
>   seem to pass by once again.

Sent along with some withered wild pinks after Major Captain of the Right Nagachika lost one of his little children

> 12
> I send these along,
> quite oversome with sadness
>   at the thought of it—
> of how the young pinks*
>   could have withered and died.

* *Nadeshiko no hana*. A group of flowers of white or pink color, including the carnation.

RS 196 (SUMMER) Once when he was living in a village deep back in the mountains, thinking forlornly that no one would ever visit him, he heard the call of a cuckoo*

13
Tell just this one thing
    to anyone who asks of me,
o cuckoo—
that at least I'm still here
    living in the world of men.[5]

* *Hototogisu*. A small bird of the cuckoo family whose plaintive song evoked memories of travelers far from home.

RS 449 (WINTER)

14
If I left this place,
would you bury every trace
    that tells I was here?
—you white snow in the garden
    of my home so long a time.[6]

NOTES

1. This poem is also included in SZKKS (no. 1693), but as an anonymous work because of the prince's involvement with the Southern Loyalists.
2. This poem is also included in SZKKS (no. 870) without attribution to the prince.
3. An allusive variation on SKKS 363, by Fujiwara no Teika. See poem 16 in the section on Fujiwara no Teika in this anthology.

4. This poem is also included in SZKKS (no. 1223) without attribution.

5. An allusive variation on KKS 152, by Mikuni no Machi (precise dates unknown) [Headnote: Topic unknown]: "Just a moment, please, / you cuckoo from the mountains. / I want to give you / this message to deliver: 'I am weary of the world.'" (*Yayoya mate / yamahototogisu / kotozutemu / ware yo no naka ni / sumiwabinu to yo.*) McCullough 1985:43.

6. An allusive variation on KKS 972, by Ariwara no Narihira [Headnote: Sent to someone at Fukakusa as he prepared to return to the capital after having lived there]: "This Fukakusa, / my home for so long a time— / if I go away, / will it become a wild field, / 'Deep Grass' deeper than ever?" (*Toshi o hete / sumikoshi sato o / idete inaba / itodo fukakusa / no to ya narinamu.*) McCullough 1985:212.

JAPANESE TEXTS

1 Kaerusa o / haya isoganan / na ni shi ou / yama no sakura wa /
   kokoro tomu to mo

2 Furusato wa / koishiku totemo / miyoshino no / hana no sakari o /
   ikaga misuten

3 Omoiyare / kiso no misaka mo / kumo tozuru / yama no konata
   no / samidare no koro

4 Asajifu no / ono no shinohara / kaze soyogi / hito shirurame ya / aki
   tachinu to wa

5 Ōhara ya / yuki furitsumite / michi mo nashi / kyō wa na yaki so /
   mine no sumigama

6 Nagametsuru / hana mo momiji mo / chirihatete / kokoro no iro
   zo / ima wa munashiki

7 Ika ni sen / tagitsu namida no / shigarami mo / kakete seku beki /
   tamoto naranu o

8 Ima zo uki / onaji miyako no / uchi nite wa / kokoro bakari no /
   hedate narishi o

9 Kono kure mo / towaremu koto wa / yomogiu no / sueba no kaze
   no / aki no hageshisa

10 Onajiku wa / tomo ni mishi yo no / hito mogana / koishisa o dani
   / katari awasen

11 Yogatari ni / tare tsutauran / oi ga mi no / tada me no mae ni / sugishi
   mukashi o

12 Yosoetsutsu / omoiyaru   koso / kanashikere / kaku   ya   shioreshi /
    nadeshiko no hana
13 Koto towamu / hito ni tsugeyo / hototogisu / ware yo no naka ni
    / ari to bakari wa
14 Idete inaba / waga ato sae ya / uzumoren / sumi koshi yado no /
    niwa no shirayuki

DEFENDERS OF
DIFFERENT FAITHS

Kazan'in Nagachika

Imagawa Ryōshun

Reizei Tamemasa

Asukai Masayori

Gyōkō

Shōtetsu

Tō no Tsuneyori

Shinkei

Sōgi

Shōhaku

Sanjōnishi Sanetaka

Kazan'in Nagachika (1345?–1429)

Prince Munenaga never saw the unification of the Northern and Southern courts. But his main poetic disciple, Kazan'in Naga-chika (also known by the sobriquet Kōun) was able to move back to the capital after a treaty ended the dispute between the two imperial factions in 1392. He spent the rest of his life there, in time gaining acceptance among fellow adherents of the Nijō tradition.

The heir of one of the *seigake*—a group of families that could ascend as high as the office of Chancellor (Daijō Daijin) in the court bureaucracy—Nagachika could have expected to distin-guish himself in rank and title, had he been born into the aris-tocracy of the Northern Court. In Yoshino, however, his relatively high offices—he went as far as Palace Minister (Nai-daijin)— meant very little. Like Prince Munenaga, he seems to have spent a great deal of time on the road before the unification of the courts. As with so many of his peers, his one consolation in all of his struggles was poetry, which he pursued avidly from his teens, finding a natural teacher in Prince Munenaga, whom he helped with the compilation of the *Shinyōshū*.

After 1392, Nagachika took the tonsure and went to live in the hills around the capital, first in a temple in the north and later in one of the subtemples of the Nanzenji. One of his broth-ers was a Zen priest, and he too was influenced by Sung phi-losophy and Zen thought.

In his last years the once expatriate became a regular at the poetry gatherings of Ashikaga Yoshimochi (1386–1428), even judging a poetry contest sponsored by the shōgun in 1414. Nagachika's poems, the most interesting of which come from his days with Prince Munenaga, are noteworthy primarily for their delicacy and, like those of his mentor, for their profound sense of the uncertainty of life. He wrote a poetic treatise, titled simply *Kōun kuden* (The Teachings of Kōun), that is now taken as a statement of the poetic theory of Prince Munenaga. (See Kubota et al. 1976:252–253, 257–578. The text of the work is available in *NKT* 5.)

Poems

SYS 190 (SUMMER) Written on the topic "Faint Cry of the Cuckoo,"*
for a three-hundred-round poem contest held at the home of the Regent

> 1
> O distant cuckoo—
> your one real call sounds so faint
>   in the gloom of night
> that it can in no way match
>   the way you sing in my dreams.

* *Hototogisu.* A small bird of the cuckoo family who is notorious for
granting the gift of its song—a harbinger of summer—only seldom,
despite the impatience of poets.

SYS 239 (SUMMER) From a five-hundred-round poem contest

> 2
> Beneath the new green
>   in the shade of a cherry tree,
> I take the evening cool—
> waiting for the breezes
>   that upset me so last spring.*

* Although welcome in summer, those same breezes threatened the
blossoms in spring.

Kazan'in Nagachika   261

SYS 662 (LOVE)[1] On "Love, with Bird as an Image," from a poem sent to the Regent's home for a three-hundred-round poem contest

3
Shall I retire now,
alone and full of longing?
—on a night cold as the frost
    on the wing-joints* of ducks
        swimming through the reeds.†[2]

* *Hagai*. The joint where the wings meet on the duck's back.
† *Ashi*. Common reeds found along ditches, inlets, swamps, etc.

SYS 830 (LOVE) Topic unknown

4
My mind on the form
    of the one who will not come,
I am up late at night—
not ready to go myself
    beneath the hesitant moon.*[3]

* *Izayoi no tsuki*. The moon of the sixteenth night—just one night after the full moon of the fifteenth—in the lunar calendar, which is said to "hesitate" *(isayou)* before appearing.

5

Thinking of the past,
I call up your fond image
    from deep in my heart—
a memento of our love
    you did not mean to leave behind.

NOTES

1. This poem is also included in SZKKS (no. 1175) under Naga-chika's priestly name of Meigi.

2. An allusive variation on MYS 64, by Prince Shiki (precise dates unknown) [Headnote: A poem written by Prince Shiki when there was an Imperial Procession to the Naniwa Palace on the ninth day of the Eleventh Month of the third year of the Kyōun era]: "Frost is falling / on the wing-joints of ducks / swimming through the reeds— / as in the cold of evening / I think of Yamato." (*Ashibe yuku / kamo no hagai ni / shimo furite / samuki yūbe wa / yamato shi omōyu.*) The third year of the Kyōun era was 706.

3. An allusive variation on KKS 690, anonymous [Headnote: Topic unknown]: "While I asked myself / whether you might be coming / or I might go there, / the hesitant moon appeared, / and I slept, the door unlocked." (*Kimi ya komu / ware ya yukamu no / isayoi ni / maki no itado mo / sasazu nenikeri.*) McCullough 1985:153.

JAPANESE TEXTS

1 Honoka naru / yami no utsutsu no / hitokoe wa / yume ni masaranu / hototogisu kana
2 Shigeriau / sakura ga shita no / yūsuzumi / haru wa ukarishi / kaze zo mataruru

3 Nagekitsutsu / hitori ya sanen / ashibe yuku / kamo no hagai mo / shimo sayuru yo ni
4 Konu hito no / omokage nagara / fukenu nari / ware ya yukamu no / izayoi no tsuki
5 Omoiidete / kokoro ni shinobu / omokage ya / hito no nokosanu / katami naruran

Imagawa Ryōshun (1326–1420)

Imagawa Ryōshun, who is known now primarily as one of the great polemicists of the liberal camp, spent most of his life as a military man. Born the son of a provincial war baron of Ashikaga lineage, he joined the forces of the shogunate as a young man, eventually becoming one of the government's leading generals. The climax of his fighting career came in 1371, when he was sent to Kyūshū to subdue an army of Southern loyalists that had managed to repulse Northern troops for years. Ryōshun, then still known by his lay name of Sadayo, succeeded where others had failed, although only after a long campaign. He stayed on as Governor-General of Kyūshū until 1395.

Ryōshun's father taught him archery and the military arts, but he also taught him poetry, which became one of his life's ruling passions.[1] In his twenties he studied under Tamemoto, the heir of Kyōgoku Tamekane, and under Reizei Tamehide. From the beginning he seems to have favored the Kyōgoku-Reizei styles, the directness of which probably appealed to him as a man of action. Another of his literary interests was linked verse, which he studied under Gusai (d. 1376?) and later under Nijō Yoshimoto. While in Kyūshū, Ryōshun gathered around him local poets and literary men from among his own staff, creating his own salon.

After returning to the capital in 1395, Ryōshun suffered a few political reverses; for a time he was even forced to flee from the capital in order to escape the wrath of the shōgun Ashikaga Yoshimitsu (1358–1408). After being pardoned, he returned to

the capital and spent the rest of his life pursuing religious de-
votions and poetry. It was at this time that he made his repu-
tation as a champion of the Reizei cause, writing a series of es-
says and petitions attacking the Nijō camp, particularly Gyōjin
(d. 1412) and Gyōkō (1391–1455), whom he saw as priestly
upstarts who should not be allowed to compete with the legit-
imate heirs of Teika—meaning, of course, Reizei Tamemasa
(1361–1417) and his sons.[2]

In his essays, Ryōshun hearkened back to Tamekane, insisting
that poetry should be a direct expression of experience.[3] His own
poems, even when they fail artistically, are always fresh and un-
adorned. His most important contribution to medieval poetry,
however, was in his tutoring of Shōtetsu (1381–1459), who be-
came the finest uta poet of the fifteenth century.

NOTES

1. Yonehara 1976:816.
2. Inoue 1984:52–53. Ryōshun's main works—*Nigonshō* (1403),
Ryōshun isshiden (1409), and *Rakusho roken* (1412)—can be found in
NKT 5.
3. *Ryōshun isshiden, NKT* 5:180.

Poems

FGS 83 (MISCELLANEOUS) Topic unknown

1
The least it could do
   is blow the scattering blossoms
     into my sleeves —
then I could at least believe
    the wind has some compassion.

FROM *TŌYASHŪ KIKIGAKI 32,* in *SKKT* 5

2
If one must live in the world
   then this is how things should be:
up till near daybreak
    lamenting the last cold rays
     of the early moon.[1]

FROM *MICHIYUKIBURI,* IN *GR* 15. From among boats in the offing, smoke was rising—from people preparing breakfast, it seemed. The sight of the smoke trailing over the waves made me wish for a person of feeling I could show it to:

> 3
> What had looked like fires
>   tended by seaweed burners
> out on the waves
>   turned out to be torches aflame
> on the boats of fisherman.

FROM *MICHIYUKIBURI,* IN *GR* 15. [Written in Nagato* as a dedication to Myōjin, God of the Sumiyoshi Shrine†]‡

> 4
> Within the sacred fence
>   grows a venerable pine—
> grown of a seed
>   from our great nation's
>   many leaves of words.

* Located at the very tip of Honshū (modern Yamaguchi Prefecture).
† A shrine located in Nagato. Sumiyoshi Myōjin was one of the patron gods of poets.
‡ For this poem and the poem which follows, the bràcketed headnote is my paraphrase of the section of the travel diary in which the poem appears.

FROM *YOSHIMITSU-KŌ ITSUKUSHIMA-MŌDE NO KI,* in *GR* 15. [Written on a boat in the Inland Sea* as they passed Iyo†]

5

So cold is the night
    that I want another layer
    of traveler's robes.
It was harsh even in spring—
this autumn wind on the bay.

---

* The sea between southern Honshū, Kyūshū, and Shikoku.
† Modern day Ehime Prefecture.

FROM *RYŌSHUN ISSHI-DEN* 10, IN *SKKT* 5. Written after these lines from Bo Juyi: "When one has a mother back home, this autumn wind brings tears."[2]

6

Even if one has
    no parent waiting back home
evening on the road
    is a time of sadness
beneath the autumn sky.

NOTES

1. An allusive variation on KKS 625, by Mibu no Tadamine. See note 2 in the section on Fujiwara no Tameuji in this anthology.
2. The line is actually from a Chinese poem by Minamoto no Tamenori. See note 13 in the section on Fujiwara no Teika in this anthology.

JAPANESE TEXTS

1 Chiru hana o / semete tamoto ni / fukitomeyo / so o dani kaze no / nasake to omowan
2 Yo ni sumaba / ge ni kaku mogana / tsurenakute / nokoru o oshimu / ariake no tsuki
3 Nami no ue ni / shio yaku ka to / mietsuru wa / ama no obune ni / taku hi narikeri
4 Kamigaki no / matsu no oigi wa / waga kuni no / yamato koto no ha no / tane ya narikemu
5 Yo o samumi / kasane ya semashi / tabigoromo / haru dani araki / aki no urakaze
6 Furusato ni / oya naki tabi no / yūgure mo / kanashikarikeru / aki no sora kana

Reizei Tamemasa (1361–1417)

Last of the important Reizei poets, Tamemasa (whose name is also read Tametada) was the great-grandson of Tamesuke, the grandson of Tamehide, and the son of Tamekuni (precise dates unknown), and thus heir to the poetic mandate at birth. He lost his father to the priestly life in childhood, however; and because he was only eleven years old at the time of Tamehide's death, he found himself unable to stand up to competition from the Nijō faction—now represented by Tameshige, nearly four decades his senior. His early years seem to have been unhappy.

Partly due to the polemical efforts of Imagawa Ryōshun, who became the younger man's champion after the death of Tameshige, Tamemasa did finally gain prominence at court around the turn of the century, eventually becoming the only Reizei heir in history to be granted the title of Major Counselor. His greatest supporter was the Ashikaga shōgun, Yoshimochi.

Although Imagawa Ryōshun can hardly be described as an objective appraiser of Tamemasa's work, Ryōshun's characterization of him as a man who composed poetry that always "sounded fresh and new" *(ana mezurushi to kikoyu),* always came from "the depths of his heart," and was never written to "gain the praise of others," seems entirely apt *(Rakusho roken, NKT* 5:191). His work has a vitality that was rare in his age.

Poems

SZKKS 424 (AUTUMN) On "An Autumn Evening," from among the poems of a hundred-poem-sequence composed for the Lay Priest and Former Prime Minister, Rokuon-In [Ashikaga Yoshimitsu]

> 1
> Loneliness
>   was something I was used to—
> or so I had thought.
> But now here it is again
>   in the autumn dusk.

SZKKS 1677 (MISCELLANEOUS) "Fireflies Over a Marsh"

> 2
> Over marsh water
>   where floating grasses
>   drift with the wind,
> fireflies are darting about—
> uncertain rays of light.

TS 82 (SPRING) "The Spring Moon Concealed"

3

When can one be sure
   that another layer of haze
      has obscured the sky?
When one's sleeves no longer glow
   with the light of the midnight moon.

TS 91 (SPRING) "A Lark Along the Road"

4

The farmer's plow
   must have left some grass unturned
      out on the meadow:
from the paddy dike up ahead
   a lark is singing.

TS 115 (SPRING) "Spring of Blossoms"

5

Down the mountain road
   come what looks like clouds—
the village people
   must be heading back home now
      with sprigs of cherry blossoms.*

* Referring to people who have broken off branches and made garlands
for their heads.

6

Was that a plover?†
I wonder, up in the night,
when a cuckoo calls.
I could be more certain
    if it would but sing once more.

---

* *Hototogisu.* A small bird of the cuckoo family that is notorious for granting the gift of its song—a harbinger of summer—only seldom, despite the impatience of poets.

† *Chidori.* Small shore birds whose plaintive cry is often employed by poets as a symbol of the loneliness usually associated with winter nights. Here the poet uses the bird's cry ironically, to suggest that he feels the same even in summer.

TS 263 (SUMMER) "Short Summer Night"

7

I called over friends,
thinking to enjoy the cool
    of the night air;
and when I looked outside again
    the moon was in the dawn sky.

TS 298 (SUMMER) "Taking the Cool in the Shade of the Trees"

> 8
> As the days go by,
> the rotting willow's shadow
>   is so slight now
> that the water I cup to drink
>   feels lukewarm in my hands.

TS 299 (SUMMER) "Taking the Cool to Forget Summer"

> 9
> My shutters open,
> I sit out on the veranda
>   in the cool of dusk;
> not yet here, autumn floats by
>   on the wind low in the pines.

TS 390 (AUTUMN) "A Snipe in the Marshes"

> 10
> This sad beauty*
>   I had thought of as coming
>   only at autumn dusk:
> a snipe rises from the marsh
>   before the moon at dawn.[1]

* *Aware*. A term referring to the sadness that adheres in things perceived by those with a sensibility attuned to the perishability of human experience.

11

The woodsman passes
    and storm winds follow behind
        to see him on his way—
leaves swirling all around
    on the rope bridge in the valley.[2]

12

"It's snowed!" I see,
opening up my shutters
    to the light of dawn—
when from next door comes the sound
    of someone doing the same thing.

13

How many times now
    have I awakened to listen?
The village people
    bustle about endlessly
        as the year comes to its end.

TS 748 (LOVE) "Love, with Spider as an Image"

> 14
> No letter comes—
> not even one proclaiming
>   his excuses:
> reeds* tied and bound by the threads
>   of a spider's web.

* *Ogi.* A large flowering grass resembling *susuki* (miscanthus) in shape and features.

TS 799 (LOVE) "Love, with Lamp as an Image"

> 15
> I would show you this:
> how the light of my lamp
>   has burnt itself down,
> while I waited for you to come—
> scenting my sleeves with its smoke.

NOTES

1. An allusive variation on SKKS 362, by Monk Saigyō. See note 6 in the section on Tonna in this anthology.

2. An allusive variation on KYS 254, by Fujiwara no Akisue (1055–1123) [Headnote: Written on the idea of falling leaves burying a bridge]: "On Mount Ogura / a storm comes down from the peak / blowing so hard / that the rope bridge in the valley / is the color of autumn leaves." (*Ogurayama / mine no arashi no / fuku kara ni / tani no kakehashi / momiji shinikeri.*)

JAPANESE TEXTS

1 Sabishisa wa / narenuru mono to / omoedomo / mata imasara no / aki no yūgure

2 Ukikusa no / kaze ni tadayou / numamizu ni / kage sadamarade / tobu hotaru kana

3 Sara ni mata / kasumeru hodo no / shiraruru wa / sode ni utsuranu / yowa no tsukikage

4 Suki ireshi / noda no shibafu ya / nokoruran / yukute no tsutsumi / hibari naku nari

5 Kudariyuku / yamaji no kumo ya / satobito no / hana ori kazashi / kaeru naruran

6 Kuina ka to / omou nezame no / hototogisu / sore ni sadamaru / hitogoe mogana

7 Suzumu tote / atari no tomo o / yobitatete / furisakemireba / tsuki no akebono

8 Higoro yori / kuchiki no yanagi / kage asami / musubu shimizu zo / nuruku narinuru

9 Mado akete / hashii suzushiki / yūgure ni / konu aki ukabu / matsu no shitakaze

10 Aware o ba / tada yūgure ni / omoishi o / shigi tatsu sawa no / ariake no tsuki

11 Yamabito no / ato ni arashi ya / okururamu / ko no ha midaruru / tani no kakehashi

12 Yuki yo tote / mado hikiakuru / akebono ni / tonari no sato mo / hito oto no shite

13 Ikutabi ka / nezamete kikedo / satobito no / itonami taenu / toshi no kure kana

14 Kagoto ni mo / tsugetaru fumi wa / mie mo sede / ogi hikimusubu / sasagani no ito

15 Misebaya na / sodeguchi itaku / takishimete / hito machifukuru / tomoshibi no kage

Asukai Masayori (1358–1428)

One of the inheritors of the conservative tradition after the demise of the main Mikohidari line was the Asukai family. Their central place in poetic history after Masatsune had been guaranteed by a marriage alliance with the Nijō family that had provided brides for Tameuji and later Tamemichi (1271–1299), who bore two of the most important Nijō poets of the fourteenth century—Tameyo and Tamesada. As in the case of Masatsune himself, the heirs of the house continued to specialize in the game of *kemari* (kickball); by the time of Nijō Tameshige's death in 1385, however, the Asukai were also one of the premier poetic houses at court (see Inoue. 1984:32–34).

Masayori, head of the house in the late 1300s and on into the next century, was a close friend of the shōgun Ashikaga Yoshimitsu, one of the most courtly of Ashikaga potentates. Together, the two men presided over a lively group of artists and poets, including not only Emperor Go-Komatsu (1377–1433) and a number of courtiers and priests—notably Gyōjin, grandson of Tonna—but also the high-class warriors of Yoshimitsu's entourage. With the unification of the Southern and Northern courts in 1392, the country had entered a rare period of peace, during which Yoshimitsu sponsored a revival of the aristocratic arts.

When Yoshimitsu took priestly orders in 1398, Masayori followed him. But neither man had any intention of truly forsaking the world. If anything, the next ten years were the most opulent of Yoshimitsu's reign. And even after the latter's death in 1408, the revival continued, with Masayori at its heart, acting as poet laureate, contest judge, and critic. His son Masayo (1390–1452), also active in these years, went on to serve as chief compiler of the *Shin zokukokinshū* (New Collection of Ancient and Modern Times Continued, 1439), last of the imperial collections of *waka*.

Although basically a conservative, Masayori was a competent poet who earned the respect not only of his fellows in the Nijō cause, but also of liberals such as Shōtetsu. His sons and grandsons presided over the final decline of the court tradition.

Poems

SZKKS 29 (SPRING) On "Haze Over the Hills"

1

Still so cold is spring
    that the wind along the coast
at Windswept Shore*
    will not allow the haze to spread
before the far peaks of Kii.†

* Fukiage no Hama. Located near the mouth of the Ki River, in Kii
(modern Wakayama Prefecture).
† The peaks of mountains inland, to the southeast.

SZKKS 1601 (LAMENTS) On the thirteenth anniversary of the death of
the Lay Priest and Former Prime Minister Rokuon-in [Ashikaga Yoshi-
imitsu], he went to the gravesite and wrote this poem, remembering
their long association as men of the same age:

2

Trees of the same age,
we shared shade until he left me—
a lone, rotting trunk.
Now, after ten years and more,
why am I still here?

Asukai Masayori   281

SZKKS 1732 (MISCELLANEOUS) Once when Masayori was very ill for a number of days, Retired Emperor Go-Komatsu sent off an Imperial Prayer for him to the Shin Tamazushima Shrine.* When Masayori seemed to get a little better, the Retired Emperor sent him this poem:

3
Is it not time now
    for the light of the moon
        to shine forth again?
—making good use of a sky
    soon to be clear of mist.

* Located in Kii (modern Wakayama City).

To which Masayori replied:

4
Now I realize:
it is my sovereign's light
    that has cleared the mist
to let me see the bright moon
    shining on me from above.

5

Has frost left last night
   now turned into beads of dew?
The hues are deeper now
   on those autumn leaves reflecting
     the light of the morning sun.*

* Dew, showers, and frost were deemed responsible for leaves changing color in autumn.

SGS 48 "Insects Near a Hut in the Fields"

6

That I am living
   in this grass hut in the fields
     is known to no one.
For whom does the pine cricket* call
   in such a consoling tone?[1]

* *Matsumushi*. A cricket who appears often in poetry because of the possibilities for punning afforded by *matsu*—meaning either pine tree or "waiting" ("pining").

7

Dusk falls with a chill
as a cloud comes down upon
treetops on the peak—
looking like snow piling up
where none has fallen at all.[2]

NOTES

1. An echo of GSS 260, by Ki no Tsurayuki [Headnote: Topic unknown]: "I know of no one / who has come to live here / in these autumn fields. / For whom does the pine cricket wait, / to call out in such full voice?" (*Aki no no ni / kiyadoru hito mo / omōezu / tare o matsumushi / kokora nakuran.*)
2. This poem may have been written by Masayori's son, Masayo.

JAPANESE TEXTS

1 Haru samumi / nao fukiage no / hamakaze ni / kasumi mo hatenu / kiji no tōyama

2 Aioi no / kage no kuchiki to / okureite / totose amari wa / nani no-koruran

3 Tsuki mo haya / yaya idenubeki / hikari kana / hareyuku kiri no / sora ni makasete

4 Ima zo shiru / kimi no hikari ni / kiri harete / mata mi o terasu / tsuki o min to wa

5 Oku shimo mo / tsuyu to narite ya / asahikage / utsuru momiji wa / iro masaruran

6 Sumu to dani / shirarenu nobe no / kusa no iori ni / tare matsu mushi no / nagusamete naku

7 Saekurete / mine no kozue ni / iru kumo ya / furade mo tsumoru / yuki to miyuran

Gyōkō (1391–1455)

A great-grandson of Tonna, Gyōkō began his career under the tutelage of his father, Gyōjin, participating in poetry contests at Yoshimitsu's court from a young age. After his father's death in 1412, he became a leader of the conservative school, first with Asukai Masayori and later with Masayo. In 1433 he was appointed Librarian of the Poetry Bureau and assigned the task of helping Masayo with the compilation of the *Shin zokukokinshū.*

In addition to his poetry, Gyōkō left two important travel diaries, both records of his journeys with the shōgun Ashikaga Yoshinori (1394–1441), one of his chief patrons. With the Ashikaga family as his supporters, he made a name for himself at court. In ecclesiastical rank he attained the position of Acting Archbishop, with his residence at Ninnaji's Jōkō-in.

Gyōkō attracted many disciples, especially from the priestly ranks and from the warrior elite. Among Reizei advocates, however, he had his critics—among them Imagawa Ryōshun and Shōtetsu, who seem to have been particularly derisive of the talents of their Nijō opponents.[1] In a poetry contest sponsored by the Former Regent Ichijō Kaneyoshi (1402–1481), also a Reizei supporter, in 1443—several years after the murder of his benefactor Ashikaga Yoshinori—Gyōkō found himself a lone conservative in a room full of liberals, who made life difficult for him for a time.[2] In truth, however, both styles were nearing the end of their sway over Japanese poetry.

NOTES

1. Inoue 1984:52–53; Inada 1978:224–252.
2. *Saki no Sesshō-ke uta-awase, ZGR* 15:255–320.

Poems

SZKKS 311 (SPRING) On "The Summer Moon in the Morning," written at the mansion of Retired Emperor Go-Komatsu when those assembled were composing a fifty-poem sequence, "searching for topics"*

1
The moonlight remains
　　on the stones beneath the eaves
　　　　for morning cleaning:
as if even in summer
　　there were frost to be swept away.

* *Dai o suguru.* An informal poem contest in which poets gathered to compose poems extemporaneously on topics written out, placed on a dais, and then chosen at random.

On "A Thin Snowfall," presented as one of the poems in a hundred-poem sequence

2
Even as it falls
    it mixes with the cogon weeds,*
looking like blossoms
    bent low under their own weight—
the year's first snow, this morning.

* *Asaji.* A short reed-like plant that grows in clumps on moorlands and meadows. In poetry, it carries a melancholy connotation and is generally shown thriving around run-down or abandoned homes.

BG 69 "Late Blossoms in Cold Mountains"

3
When will it break loose
    the bonds holding the flowers?
The valley breeze
    for now carries only
        the sound of breaking ice.[1]

BG 125 "Summer Grasses in the Fields at Dusk"

4

Even on the plumes
    of the flowering miscanthus*
        the dew has fallen:
the evening wind on the fields
    is beckoning autumn to come.

* *Susuki*. A large plant resembling pampas grass that flowers each autumn in hills and fields.

BG 130 "Wisteria in the Rain"

5

Even the pond water
    seems to take on deep color—
carried along
    by waves of rain falling down
        over plumes of wisteria.*

* *Fuji*. The "royal" flower of Japan, because of its rich purple color and association with the Fujiwara family. Here the rain falling on the delicate plumes of the flower takes some blossoms with it as it enters the pond.

BG 200 On "The Moon Coming Up from Behind the Hills," from a group of three poems written for the monthly poetry meeting of Shigenari Ason

6

The brilliant moon
   rising into the deep blue
of the boundless sky
   finds a first home* for its light
in the pine boughs on the peak.

* The moon is said to "take lodging in" things that reflect its light: water, dew, etc.

BG 306 "The Moon from a Boat"

7

Not satisfied
   with the expanse of the waves,
the moon takes lodging
   in tiny drops of water
      falling from the boatman's pole.*

* Punt poles *(sao)* were used to push flatboats *(takasebune)* through pools.

BG 414 "The Moon"

8
Right before my eyes
    those unchanging rays
        undergo a change:
moving past gaps in the clouds
    is the moon this autumn night.[2]

GHN 47 "Mist"

9
A moonlit night:
around the unclear shapes
    of the pine branches,
the mists begin to gather,
blown by the autumn wind.

GHN 50 "Travel"

10
O for a pathway
    that could take me back
        to my distant home!
There is no end in sight
    on the floating bridge of dreams.[3]

NOTES

1. An allusive variation combining two KKS poems—KKS 12, by Minamoto Masazumi (precise dates unknown) [Headnote: A poem from the Empress' Contest during the reign of the Kanpyō Emperor]: "Might they perhaps be / the first blossoms of springtime— / those waves bursting forth / through each crevice in the ice / melting in the valley breeze?" (*Tanikaze ni / tokuru kōri no / hima goto ni / uchiizuru nami ya / haru no hatsuhana*); and KKS 246, anonymous [Headnote: Topic unknown]: "To my heart's content / I propose to dally here / in these autumn fields / where blossoms untie their cords. / Pray do not find fault with me." (*Momokusa no / hana no himo toku / aki no no ni / omoitawaremu / hito na togame so*). McCullough 1985:16, 61.

2. An allusive variation on SCSS 294, by Kojijū (late Heian period) [Headnote: Written when the Gokyōgoku Regent commissioned hundred-poem sequences]: "How many times now / have I seen autumn come round / and then pass away? / —looking up at the rays / of the unchanging moon." (*Iku meguri / sugiyuku aki ni / ainuramu / kawaranu tsuki no / kage o nagamete.*)

3. An allusion to the final chapter of *The Tale of Genji*, titled "The Floating Bridge of Dreams," and probably also to Teika's famous poem alluding to the same material. See poem 12 in the section on Fujiwara no Teika in this anthology and Seidensticker 1976, 2:1080–1090.

JAPANESE TEXTS

1 Tsuki mo nao / nokoru migiri no / asakiyome / natsu sae shimo o / harau to zo miru

2 Furu hodo mo / asaji ni majiri / saku hana no / nabiku to zo miru / kesa no hatsuyuki

3 Hana no himo / itsu fukitokan / tanikaze wa / kōri kudakishi / oto bakari shite

4 Ho ni idenu / susuki ga ure mo / tsuyu chirite / aki o zo maneku / nobe no yūkaze

5 Ikemizu no / iro sae fukashi / ame fureba / sakisou fuji no / nami ni hikarete

6 Kagiri naki / sora no midori ni / sumu tsuki mo / mazu kage yadosu / mine no matsugae

7 Kagiri naki / namiji ni akade / sasu sao no / shizuku ni sae mo / tsuki zo yadoreru

8 Miru mama ni / kawaranu kage no / kawaru kana / kumoma o meguru / aki no yo no tsuki
9 Yūzukuyo / sadaka ni mo naki / matsu no ha ni / nao kiri mayou / akikaze zo fuku
10 Furusato ni / kayou bakari no / michi mogana / sue mo tsuzukanu / yume no ukihashi

Shōtetsu (1381–1459)

Although born in the provinces, Shōtetsu came to the capital with his parents at around age ten and spent most of his life there, studying poetry under both Imagawa Ryōshun and Reizei Tamemasa. He took the tonsure—although for what reason we do not know—in 1414 and spent some years as a scribe at Tōfukuji, one of the great Zen establishments of the time. But even during his time as an active cleric, he was known primarily as a poet whose major patrons were the great warrior houses.

Shōtetsu inherited Imagawa Ryōshun's role as defender of the Reizei line after the latter's death in 1420. Sadly, however, his affiliation with the liberal cause, rather than working to his credit, led to his being ostracized by the shōgun Yoshinori—a supporter of the Asukai family—in the mid-1430s. Angered over some incident that history has not disclosed, Yoshinori confiscated the poet's estate rights around 1435, and for a time thereafter, the name of Shōtetsu ceased to appear on the roles of government poetry gatherings. When the *Shin zokukokinshū* was presented for imperial review in 1439, none of his poems was included.[1]

After the assassination of Yoshinori in 1441, Shōtetsu regained his rightful place in poetic circles. At court, he was supported by Ichijō Kaneyoshi and the Reizei family, and his friends in the military houses also welcomed his return. Before long he had collected an impressive number of disciples, including the linked-verse poets Chiun (d. 1448), Sōzei (d. 1455), and Shinkei (1406–1475), as well as a number of poets who went on to gain prominence in the older uta form. His personal collection, *Sōkonshū* (A Collection of Grasses and Roots), which contains over ten thousand poems, shows that he was one of the premier figures of his day even in the chambers of the mighty. Although his poetry was criticized by Gyōkō and others, even his rivals admitted his talent.[2]

Shōtetsu's profound respect for Fujiwara no Teika above all other poets is clearly indicated in his own critical works and those of his disciples.[3] And his poetry too is reminiscent of Teika's in its rhetorical complexity, intensity, and richness of imagery and conception. Most modern critics consider Shōtetsu the last truly great uta poet of the court tradition.

NOTES

1. Inada 1978:51–63.
2. Inada 1978:5 6.
3. See *Shōtetsu monogatari, NKBT* 65:166; *Tōyashū kikigaki, NKT* 5:417; and *Oi no kurigoto, NST* 23:417.

Poems

SOKS 230 "White Hydrangeas"

1
The way stretches far
   beneath branches dense with new growth
      in the gloom of dusk;
but I am kept on my path—
by white hydrangeas* in bloom.

* *Unohana*. A shrub related to the hydrangea, with white flowers that bloom in early summer.

SOKS 243 "Early Autumn"

2
Its sound today
   strikes my heart with no more force
      than it has before:
always it laments the sad world—
this first autumn wind.

3
Its owner moved out,
and now what's left of his hut
    is falling over.
How lonely are the bare fields!
—with harsh winds all around.

SOKS 1202 "Blossoms Falling in a Dawn Garden"

4
Moonlight visiting
    a garden where blossoms scatter
        on blustery wind—
taking lodging as transient
    as the dew glistening at dawn.

SOKS 1974 "Wind of an Evening Shower" Written at his monthly poetry meeting, on the twenty-fifth day of the month

5
Up above the winds
    of a passing evening shower
that roars through the fields
    withering all in its way—
You clouds! You driven leaves!

6

The autumn sunlight
   shines weaker than the thread
a spider might weave
   in wind from dark cloud banners*
fluttering over the reeds.†[1]

* *Kumo no hatate.* An archaic term for trailing clouds.
† *Ogi.* A large flowering grass resembling *susuki* (miscanthus) in shape and features.

7

With no wind blowing
   to make me doubt what I hear,
I sit inside
   listening to blossoms fall
     against my paper window.

SOKS 3011 "Plums by the Window, with Snow Falling"

8
Over my pillow
   I catch a scent so cold—
of blossoming plum
     borne past my snow-closed shutters*
      on the northern wind.[2]

* Shutters closed against the cold of the snow outside.

SOKS 3300 "Cool Beneath the Summer Moon"

9
Those upturned leaves
   high up on the swaying reeds
    look so like frost—
there's no summer in the wind
   with moonlight in my garden!

SOKS 3986 "Snow on the Mountain at Dusk"

10
Still hanging back,
the clouds too seem hesitant
   to cross at evening
over the untrodden snow
   of the rope bridge on the peak.*

* *Kakehashi*. A rope bridge spanning a mountain gorge.

"Leaves Making a Sound as They Fall"

11
From above my bed
   comes the sound of something
     heavier than rain:
after a heavy frost,
leaves scatter on the wind.

SOKS 4324 "Waiting for Love"

12
Until dawn I wait
   on a pillow rich with the scent
     of one who slept here—
suppressing the love I feel
   still burning in my breast.

SOKS 4403

13
I speak to her
   as I would to anyone—
or so I had thought.
But the true colors of my heart
   seem to have shone through.

14
Toward dusk last night
   I thought I saw the dim form
      of the one I love—
now brought to mind again
   by haze around the dawn moon.[3]

SOKS 4861 "Evening Bell"[x]

15
The hue of nightfall
   has infused itself
      deep into my heart—
wafted my way on echoes
   from the fading temple bell.

* [*Irai no*] *kane.* Rung at temples each evening at around 6 P.M.

SOKS 4962 "A Heron Standing in a River"

16
Is he in the shoals
   going after the big ones
      even in his dreams?
—that heron near the water's edge,
standing there, asleep.

17
So cold is the wind
    that a passing traveler
stops along the road
    to gulp some before going on—
sweet *sake* at a market town.

SOKS 5059 "Dream"

18
It was long ago
    when I first began to be old
        that dawn found me awake;
and now the dreams too have ended
    that used to help in early night.*

* In other words, now he is awake not only at dawn, but also in the early night, a time when he once could count upon dreams to lead him into sleep.

SOKS 5256 "Winter Bell"

19
Somehow it sounds
    much closer than usual
        in the cold clear night:
even the frost resounds
    with the tolling of the bell.*

* [Iriai no] kane.

SOKS 5809 "Night Bell* on the Mountain"

20
What a noise they make
    in the groves up on the peak
as night settles in
    and the bell-sound fades away:
the birds, the storm winds!

* [Iria no] kane.

SOKS 6974 "Distant Love"

21
So long was the road
    leading to him in my dreams
        that I woke too soon—
with the grass beneath my feet
    still rustling in my breast.[4]

SOKS 7209 " A Man Walking Through the Snow"

22
Coming toward me
    against a hard driving wind,
the man says nothing—
but I hear him tread the snow
    going down the frozen road.

SOKS 7601 "Bird"

23
One cannot be sure
    that life will last till evening—
but still I live on,
kept in the world like a white bird
    pulled along on mountain wind.

SOKS 7784 "Spring Moon in Lingering Cold"

24
In the chill of night,
the melting snow makes a sound
    as it hits the stones—
dripping from an icicle
    with the falling moonbeams.

SOKS 8323 "Plovers* at the Inlet"

25

They landed, then flew off
   amid the spray of a wave
      on Yura Inlet†—
crossing plovers that left
   only their calls behind.

* *Chidori*. Small shore birds whose plaintive cry is often employed by
poets as a symbol of winter loneliness.
† Located on the coast of Kii (modern Wakayama Prefecture).

SOKS 8512 "Dew on Lotus"

26

Morning dew gathers
   and then spills over in a stream
from a lotus leaf
      like a long string of jewels
white as sleeves of hemp.

SOKS 8685 "Paddy House"

27

I keep watch alone
   from a hut in winter fields;
and even my scarecrow
      you tear into tatters—
you rain, you storm winds!

SOKS 9161 "Falling Leaves Before the Wind"

28
I listen to the wind—
to the sound of leaves from the peak
    blown into the sky
and then left there one by one
    to fall to earth below.

SOKS 9392 "A Lament"

29
I have grown old.
What chance would I have
    to mix with people,
had I not embarked upon
    the Way of Poetry?

SOKS 11008 "Hawking"

30
Beyond the fences
    of the mountain village,
in the deep grasses,
a hunter calls to his dog
    and then heads into the fields.

31

A monkey cries out
    from its rock hut in deep hills
       held fast by clouds;
the rain makes a ruckus
    in the leaves of the scrub oak.

FROM *NANDAI WAKA*[5] "Red Leaves on a Buried Tree"*

32

Down in the valley,
a buried stump covered with vines—
for how many years
    has it put forth autumn colors
      on leaves not its own?

* From a series of poems on "difficult topics."

[A LOVE POEM][6]

33

Just a glimpse I had,
between the slats of my blinds:
till snow filled the gap—
blown along the eaves outside
    by a gust of evening wind.

NOTES

1. An echo of KKS 484, anonymous [Headnote: Topic unknown]: "For love of someone / as remote as the heavens, / I muse in the dusk, / my thoughts vagrant as dark clouds / forming their fleeting banners." (*Yūgure wa / kumo no hatate ni / mono zo omou / amatsusora naru / hito o kou tote.*) McCullough 1985:484.

2. An allusion to WRS 2, a poem in Chinese by Fujiwara no Atsumochi (late tenth century) [Headnote: Thoughts on the first day of spring, presented to the court literati in the Bureau of Letters]: "Ice on the pond's east edge is melting—on passing wind; but plum blossoms by my window on the north are still cold—bound with snow."

3. An allusion to a scene from the "Writing Practice" chapter of *The Tale of Genji,* in which Ukifune, now a nun, finds herself composing a similarly nostalgic poem while reminiscing on her past affair with Kaoru. See Seidensticker 1976, 2:1076.

4. An echo of a poem by Monk Saigyō (*Sankashū* 139) [Headnote: Written when people were composing on the topic "Blossoms Falling in a Dream" at the home of the Kamo Virgin]: "In a dream I saw / the winds of spring scattering / the cherry blossoms— / and after I woke, that sound / was still rustling in my breast." (*Harukaze no / hana o chirasu to / miru yume wa / samete mo / sawagu narikeri.*)

5. Quoted in Inada 1978:1129.

6. From a sequence of love poems. Quoted in Inada 1978:837.

JAPANESE TEXTS

1 Shigeriau / ko no shita tōki / yūyama ni / michi wa madowazu / sakeru unohana

2 Wakite kyō / mi ni shimimasaru / oto mo nashi / itsumo ukiyo no / aki no hatsukaze

3 Sumisutete / nokoru io mo / katabukinu / karita sabishiki / yomo no arashi ni

4 Tsuki zo tou / niwa no arashi ni / chiru hana no / yadori munashiki / akatsuki no tsuyu

5 Fukishiori / nowaki o narasu / yūdachi no / kaze no ue naru / kumo yo konoha yo

6 Aki no hi wa / ito yori yowaki / sasagani no / kumo no hatate ni / ogi no uwakaze

7 Magiru beki / kaze sae fukade / chirikakaru / hana no oto kiku / mado
   no uchi kana
8 Makura tou / nioi mo samushi / saku ume no / yuki ni tojitaru / mado
   no kitakaze
9 Fukikaesu / ogi no uwabe o / shimo to mite / kaze ni natsu naki /
   niwa no tsukikage
10 Waterikane / kumo mo yūbe o / nao tadoru / ato naki yuki no / mine
   no kakehashi
11 Neya no ue ni / ame yori omoki / koe su nari / shimo oku nochi
   ya / konoha chiruran
12 Machiakasu / hito no neshi yo no / makura ka ni / kogaruru mune
   o / nao osaetsutsu
13 Yo no tsune no / hito ni mono iu / yoshi nagara / omou kokoro
   no / iro ya miyuramu
14 Yūmagure / sore ka to mieshi / omokage mo / kasumu zo katami /
   ariake no tsuki
15 Yūgure no / kokoro no iro a / some zo oku / tsukihatsuru kane
   no / koe no nioi ni
16 Asase yuku / isana toru to ya / yume ni sae / migiwa no sagi no /
   nemuritachi ma wa
17 Kaze samumi / tabi naru hito mo / michiburi ni / nomisutete
   yuku / ichi no ajisake
18 Akatsuki no / nezame wa oi no / mukashi made / yoi no ma
   tanomu / yume mo taeniki
19 Tsune yori mo / chikaku kiku kane / sayuru yo no / shimo koso kane
   no / hibiki narikere
20 Sawagu nari / mine no hayashi no / yumagure / tsukidasu kane ni /
   tori mo arashi mo
21 Omoine no / yumeji o tōmi / sameyukeba / wakekoshi mune ni /
   sawagu sasahara
22 Kuru hito no / mukau fubuki ni / mono iwade / yuki fumu oto
   no / sayuru michinobe
23 Yūgure o / matsu ni inochi o / shiratori no / toba ni ukiyo o / sasou
   yamakaze
24 Sayuru yo no / yuki no shizuku wa / oto tatete / noki no taruhi ni
   / otsuru tsukikage
25 Ori ireba / iso utsu nami ni / tamayura no / towataru chidori / koe
   zo nokoreru
26 Asatsuyu no / marobiau ma ni / shirotae no / tama no o nagaku /
   otsuru hasu no ha
27 Fuyu no ta ni / hitori iomori / sōzu sae / waga mi areyuku / ame yo
   arashi yo
28 Kaze kikeba / mine no konoha no / nakazora ni / fukisuterarete /
   otsuru koegoe

29 Oihatenu / ikade ka hito ni / majirawamu / kono shikishima no /
    michi ni irazu wa
30 Yamazato no / kakio no hoka no / fukakaya ni / inu yobikoshite /
    iruru karibito
31 Saru sakebu / miyama no iwaya / kumo tojite / kozue ni sawagu /
    shii no ha no ame
32 Tsuta kakaru / tani no umoregi / iku aki ka / ono ga ha narade /
    momiji shinuran
33 Sukikage no / honoka narishi mo / chiru yuki no / kozu no ma
    uzumu / noki no yūkaze

The End of a Tradition

In the latter half of the fifteenth century, several attempts were made to publish another imperial anthology of uta, but without success. Although the Asukai and Reizei families continued to pursue the Way of Poetry for some generations—the latter in fact continuing down to the present—they did so as guardians of what was essentially a moribund art.

There was some vitality left in the genre, however. For it was in these years that poets of *renga*, linked verse, began to gain prominence in the court tradition. Such were Shinkei (1406–1475), Sōgi (1421–1502), and Shōhaku (1443–1527). All were in one way or another connected to the Nijō and Reizei factions, but together they represent more than anything else a trend away from the old conventions and toward an aesthetic influenced by the vocabulary and thematics of linked verse and *haikai*.

Shinkei was a student of Shōtetsu who spent much of his life as a cleric of high rank (Gon-Daisōzu, or "Provisional Major Bishop") but also pursued the Way of Poetry, meaning in his case both linked verse and the uta. Although at court he was never a major figure, scholars now regard him as one of the age's finest literary talents. His *Sasamegoto* (Whisperings) is one of the most original and important of late medieval poetic treatises.

Among Shinkei's students were a number of important renga poets, chief among them being Sōgi, a man of obscure background who, in the topsy-turvy world of the late Muromachi period, was able to attain great status in the literary world not only through his work in renga but also in the old uta form. His major role in the court circles of the last decades of the fifteenth century is itself a commentary on the decline of aristocratic privilege.

By training and disposition Sōgi was a conservative who maintained close ties with the warrior-poet Tō no Tsuneyori (1402–1484) and with the Asukai—ties that one of his lowly origins would have found difficult to make in earlier generations. His own student Shōhaku, on the other hand, actually came from an aristocratic family, the Nakanoin, which he left behind in order to ply his trade among merchants and warrior clans—so far had the old families fallen in worldly fortune.

A final poet deserving of mention is Sanjōnishi Sanetaka (1455–1537), scion of a major court family when those families were reduced to near penury after the Ōnin War of 1467–1477. A student of Sōgi and inheritor of Ichijō Kaneyoshi's reputation as a scholar, Sanetaka belonged to the generation that saw the court society of the last three centuries come to its end. His is a good name with which to end a survey of late medieval poetry.

Poems

Tō no Tsuneyori

TTS 84

1

In a mountain stream
    waves course over the boulders
with a sound as clear
    as the high peak is obscure
beneath clouds of summer rain.

Shinkei

JW 107 "Wild Geese Lingering on an Inlet"

2

The hour has grown late.
Away out on the inlet
    the setting moon shines
on ice where one wild-goose cry
    just fell to earth in the night.[1]

GDSS 47 [During recent battles in this province many people drowned in this river. Among them were some whom I saw regularly, so I have often come out to the riverbank to gaze up at the moon.]*

3
Now only the moon
    floats in their remembrance
        on the River Ki†—
with white crested waves to mark
    the graves of those who drowned.

* The headnote is taken from *Shinkei hyakushu waka*. The Ki runs from central Yamato (modern Nara Prefecture) into the sea in northern Kii (modern Wakayama).

GDSS 301 "Plum Blossoms Late at Night"

4
In the depths of night,
a scent of plum blossom
    wakes me from my dreams—
borne to my eaves on a breeze
    too soft to flutter my blinds.

5
Those who lift the sword
   to cut down their fellow men
meet this end—to be
firewood along the path
   over the Mountain of Death.*

* *Shide no yama.* A mountain in Buddhist Hell that all sinners must
scale as punishment for their evil acts in this life.

Sōgi

FROM *SHIRAKAWA KIKŌ.* . . . In the midst of this withered scene,
I caught sight of some bamboo grass bent low under the weight of dew,
which called to mind a poem by the Minister of the Right[2] and gave
me more of a feeling for the place. Yet, as I looked back, my thoughts
were mostly sad ones.

6
No more lamenting!
Rather submit to the dews
   of the Nasu Moor†
and know that in this world
   all are on a sad journey.

* For documentation, see "Waka Treatises" section of bibliography.
† Located in modern Fukushima Prefecture.

7

My pathway breaks off—
with no one to sweep away
    the scattered leaves
strewn before the valley door,
hidden from the evening sun.

SŌGIS 166 On "Waterfowl," composed for a thirty-poem sequence

8

Can't you see it there,
in the gulls afloat on the bay?
—a quieter world
    amid the rising clamor
        of the wild ducks in the reeds.[3]

Shōhaku

SM 189 "On a Journey"

9

Those village children
    tossed off their parting words
        so casually—
and yet how they amuse us
    as we chat along our way!

10
Even the bluster
    of the passing wind has died—
leaving the fireflies
    rising ever so quietly
        in the gloom of the dusk sky.

Sanjōnishi Sanetaka

SAISS 1753 In a dream, Ietaka commanded him to compose a poem on
"Reminiscing, with Plovers* Late at Night." At the very moment he
had thought of these lines, he awakened.

11
My thoughts on the past,
I am up till late at night—
when a plover
    from the frost-chilled riverbed
        lets out a plaintive cry.[4]

* *Chidori*. A small shore bird whose plaintive cry is often used by poets
as a symbol of winter loneliness

12
Both blossoms and trees
are obscured by the green haze
in my garden court—
here and there made white
by the moon in the dawn sky.

NOTES

1. An allusive variation on SKKS 503, by Archbishop Jien [Headnote: On "Hearing Wild Geese before the Moon," presented as part of a fifty-poem sequence]: "At Ōe Mountain / the setting moon is shining / with cold rays— / as in Toba's paddies wild geese / descend to earth in the night." (*Ōeyama / katabuku tsuki no / kage saete / tobada no omo ni / otsuru karigane.*)

2. An allusion to a poem from the personal anthology (*Kinkaishū* 348) of Minamoto no Sanetomo (1192–1219), the third Kamakura shōgun [Headnote: "Hail"]: "A fighting man / straightens arrows in his quiver / with one backstretched hand— / hail glancing from his wristguard / onto Nasu's grassy moor." (*Mononofu no / yanami tsukurou / kote no ue ni / arare tabashiru / nasu no shinohara.*)

3. An allusive variation on SKKS 1708, by Ōnakatomi no Yoshinobu (d. 991) [Headnote: Topic unknown]: "Like grass swaying / in wind from the flapping wings / of wild ducks in the reeds— / so is this uncertain world: / and on whom can one depend?" (*Ashigamo no / hakaze ni nabiku / ukikusa no / sadame naki yo o / tare ka tanoman.*)

4. An allusive variation combining lines from SKKS 201, by Fujiwara no Shunzei (see note 3 in the section on Yoshida no Kenkō in this anthology), and MYS 925, by Yamabe no Akahito (early eighth century): "Black as leopard-flower seeds / is the ever deepening night; in the *hisaki* trees / lining the pure river bed / plovers call, again and again." (*Nubatama no / yo no fukeyukeba / hisaki ouru / kiyoki kawara ni / chidori shiba naku.*)

JAPANESE TEXTS

Tō no Tsuneyori

1 Yamakawa ya / iwa kosu nami no / oto shiruku / harenu takane
no / samidare no kumo

Shinkei

2 Fukenikeri / katabuku tsuki mo / tōki e no / kōri ni otsuru / kari no
hitokoe
3 Tsuki nomi zo / katami ni ukabu / ki no kawa ya / shizumishi hito
no / ato no shiranami
4 Fukaki yo no / ume no nioi ni / yume samete / kosu makiaenu / noki
no harukaze
5 Katana mote / hito o kiru mi no / hate ya tada / shide no yamaji
ni / somagi naramashi

Sōgi

6 Nagekaji yo / kono yo wa tare mo / ukitabi to / omoinasu no no /
tsuyu ni makasete
7 Michi taete / harau hito naki / tani no to no / yūhigakure ni / chiru
konoha kana
8 Kamome uku / irie ni mizu ya / ashigamo no / sawagu naka ni
mo / shizuka naru yo o

Shōhaku

9 Sato no ko no / tada iisutekoshi / koto no ha o / tabi no susabi ni
/ katarite zo yuku
10 Fukimayou / kaze sae taete / tobu hotaru / shizuka ni noboru /
yūyama no sora

Sanjōnishi Sanetaka

11 Mukashi omou / yo no fukeyukeba / shimo samuki / kawara no
chidori / urabirete naku

12 Hana mo ki mo / midori ni kasumu / niwa no mo ni / muramura
shiroki / ariake no tsuki

APPENDIX

Genealogies

On the Twenty-One Imperial Collections

Branches of the Mikohidari House and Their Artistic Offshoots

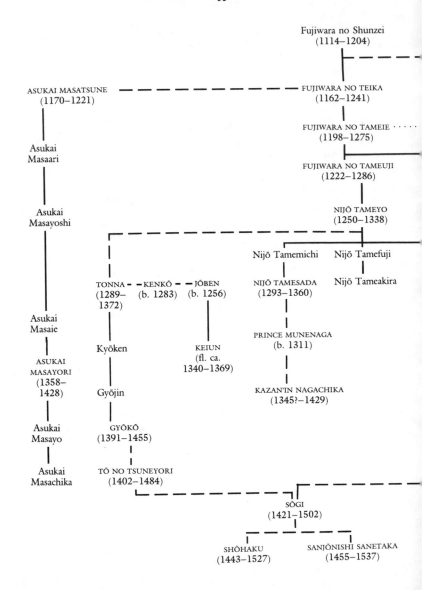

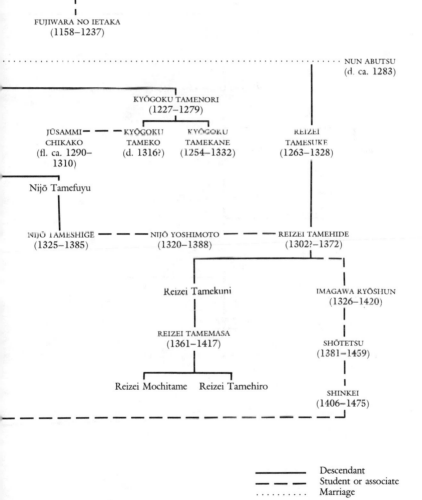

FUJIWARA NO IETAKA
(1158–1237)

NUN ABUTSU
(d. ca. 1283)

KYŌGOKU TAMENORI
(1227–1279)

JŪSAMMI
CHIKAKO
(fl. ca. 1290–
1310)

KYŌGOKU
TAMEKO
(d. 1316?)

KYŌGOKU
TAMEKANE
(1254–1332)

REIZEI
TAMESUKE
(1263–1328)

Nijō Tamefuyu

NIJŌ TAMESHIGE
(1325–1385)

NIJŌ YOSHIMOTO
(1320–1388)

REIZEI TAMEHIDE
(1302?–1372)

Reizei Tamekuni

IMAGAWA RYŌSHUN
(1326–1420)

REIZEI TAMEMASA
(1361–1417)

SHŌTETSU
(1381–1459)

Reizei Mochitame   Reizei Tamehiro

SHINKEI
(1406–1475)

——————— Descendant
— — —   Student or associate
.... Marriage

The Jimyō-In and Daikakuji Lines of the Imperial House

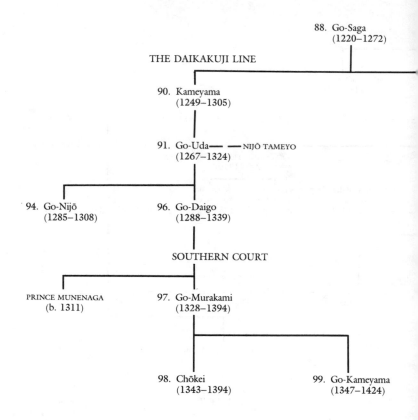

88. Go-Saga
(1220–1272)

THE DAIKAKUJI LINE

90. Kameyama
(1249–1305)

91. Go-Uda —— —— NIJŌ TAMEYO
(1267–1324)

94. Go-Nijō
(1285–1308)

96. Go-Daigo
(1288–1339)

SOUTHERN COURT

PRINCE MUNENAGA
(b. 1311)

97. Go-Murakami
(1328–1394)

98. Chōkei
(1343–1394)

99. Go-Kameyama
(1347–1424)

THE JIMYŌ-IN LINE

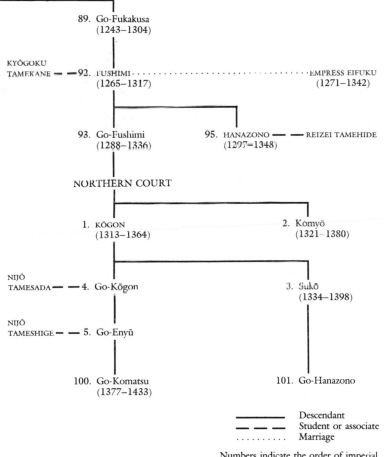

89. Go-Fukakusa
(1243–1304)

KYŌGOKU
TAMEKANE — — 92. FUSHIMI · EMPRESS EIFUKU
(1265–1317)   (1271–1342)

93. Go-Fushimi   95. HANAZONO — — REIZEI TAMEHIDE
(1288–1336)   (1297–1348)

NORTHERN COURT

1. KŌGON   2. Kōmyō
(1313–1364)   (1321–1380)

NIJŌ
TAMESADA — — 4. Go-Kōgon   3. Sukō
(1334–1398)

NIJŌ
TAMESHIGE — — 5. Go-Enyū

100. Go-Komatsu   101. Go-Hanazono
(1377–1433)

—————— Descendant
— — —   Student or associate
· · · · · · · · · · Marriage

Numbers indicate the order of imperial
succession, beginning with Go-Saga,
the 88th emperor of Japan.

On the Twenty-One Imperial Collections

The Japanese court tradition produced twenty-one imperially commissioned collections of poetry (twenty-two counting *Shin'yōshū*). Below is a list of these collections, with background information concerning those (1 and 8–21) of most importance in this book. (All numbers refer to texts in *SKKT*.)

1 *Kokinshū* (Collection of Ancient and Modern Times, 905). Compiled on the order of Emperor Daigo (885–930) by four courtiers, most prominent among them the poet, scholar, and critic Ki no Tsurayuki (872–946), who also wrote its famous Japanese preface. 1,111 poems. Chinese preface by Ki no Yoshimochi (d. 919). In almost every way imaginable—from its organization of poems into books on spring, summer, autumn, winter, felicitations, travel, love, and miscellaneous topics, to its insistence on poetry of formal elegance—this collection became the foundation for all that was to follow in later history. As such, it was virtually memorized by all aspiring poets.

2 *Gosenshū* (Later Collection, ca 951). Compiled on the order of Emperor Murakami (966–1041). 1,351 poems. No prefaces.

3 *Shūishū* (Collection of Gleanings, ca. 1006). Compiled on the order of Retired Emperor Kazan (968–1008) by Fujiwara no Kintō (966–1041). 1,351 poems. No prefaces.

4 *Goshūishū* (Later Collection of Gleanings, 1086). Compiled on the order of Retired Emperor Shirakawa (1053–1129) by Fujiwara no Michitoshi (1047–1099), who also wrote the Japanese preface. 1218 poems. No Chinese preface.

5 *Kin'yōshū* (Collection of Golden Leaves, 1124–1126). Compiled on the order of Retired Emperor Shirakawa by Minamoto no Toshiyori (sometimes called Shunrai; 1055–1129). 650 poems. No prefaces.

6　*Shikashū* (Collection of Verbal Flowers, ca. 1151–1154). Compiled on the order of Retired Emperor Sutoku (1119–1164) by Fujiwara no Akisuke (1090–1155). 415 poems. No prefaces.

7　*Senzaishū* (Collection of a Thousand Years, 1188). Compiled on the order of Retired Emperor Go-Shirakawa (1127–1192) by Fujiwara no Shunzei (sometimes called Toshinari), who also wrote the Japanese preface. 1,288 poems. No Chinese preface. Highly admired by poets of the Nijō line.

8　*Shin kokinshū* (New Collection of Ancient and Modern Times, 1206). Compiled on the order of Retired Emperor Go-Toba (1180–1239) by Fujiwara no Teika, Fujiwara no Ietaka, Fujiwara no Ariie (1155–1216), Monk Jakuren (d. 1202), Minamoto no Michitomo (1171–1227), and Asukai Masatsune, with Minamoto no Ienaga (d. 1234) as librarian. 1,978 poems. Japanese preface by Fujiwara no Yoshitsune (1169–1206). Chinese preface by Hino Chikatsuna. The most important of all the imperial anthologies after *Kokinshū*, whose name the compilers borrowed as a way to announce their high aspirations. A showcase for the formal, elegant, and richly conceived poetry favored by Go-Toba, as well as for the highly evocative and rhetorically complex poetry of the young Teika.

9　*Shin chokusenshū* (New Imperial Collection, 1234). Compiled on the order of Retired Emperor Go-Horikawa (1212–1234) by Fujiwara no Teika, who also wrote the Japanese preface. 1,374 poems. No Chinese preface. A product of Teika's later years that displays his *ushin* style. Highly admired by poets of the Nijō line.

10　*Shoku gosenshū* (Later Collection Continued, 1251). Compiled on the order of Retired Emperor Go-Saga (1220–1272) by Fujiwara no Tameie. 1,371 poems. No prefaces. Continuation of the same approach used by Teika in the *Shin chokusenshū*. Highly valued by poets of the Nijō line.

11　*Shoku kokinshū* (Collection of Ancient and Modern Times Continued, 1265). Compiled on the order of Retired Emperor Go-Saga by Fujiwara no Tameie, with the order first coming to him alone (in 1259), and later (in 1262) also to Fujiwara no Motoie (1203–1280), Kujō Ieyoshi (1192–1264), Rokujō Yukiie (1223–1275), and the monk Shinkan (1203–1276)—all opponents to the Mikohidari house who were forced on Tameie by the sixth Kamakura shōgun, Prince Munetaka

(1242–1274). 1,915 poems. Authorship of Japanese and Chinese prefaces uncertain. The finished product—which is dominated by poems of the Shinkokin era and also includes a number of pseudoarchaic poems from the *Man'yōshū*—shows that Tameie failed to triumph over his rivals.

12 *Shoku shūishū* (Collection of Gleanings Continued, 1278). Compiled on the order of Retired Emperor Kameyama (1249–1305) by Fujiwara no Tameuji, with Minamoto no Kaneuji (d. 1278?) and later the monk Keiyu (a son of Tameie, d. 1305?) as librarians. 1459 poems. No prefaces. Dominated by the plain style of the Nijō line. Criticized by some for its inclusion of poems by Tameuji's in-laws who were members of the Utsunomiya family, a warrior clan of the East Country.

13 *Shin gosenshū* (New Later Collection, 1303). Compiled on the order of Retired Emperor Go-Uda (1267–1324) by Nijō Tameyo and a number of assistants, including Tameyo's son Tamefuji and two members of the Tsumori family of Settsu province—Tameyo's in-laws. 1,607 poems. Another Nijō/Daikakuji collection that was criticized for including poems by a number of warrior clans, most chiefly the Utsunomiya and the Tō.

14 *Gyokuyōshū* (Collection of Jeweled Leaves, 1313). Compiled on the order of Retired Emperor Fushimi by Kyōgoku Tamekane. 2800 poems. No prefaces. After a failed attempt by Emperor Fushimi to sponsor an anthology in 1293, hopes for a Kyōgoku-Reizei collection seemed doomed. But with the ascension of Emperor Hanazono in 1308 another opportunity presented itself—during a period in which the unorthodox faction was in a stronger position politically than it had ever been before. Plans in 1293 had perforce demanded participation by Nijō representatives as well as Tamekane; now he was allowed by the shogunate to go on with the project alone. He began in 1311, presenting his work—the largest of all the imperial collections—just a year later, and then making final corrections in 1313. From the beginning the project was a partisan one, making the anthology a clear statement of the unorthodox school, with the Jimyō-In and Kyōgoku-Reizei circles dominant in every way. Also well represented are poets of the Shinkokin era.

15 *Shoku senzaishū* (Collection of a Thousand Years Continued, 1318–1320). Compiled on the order of Retired Emperor Go-Uda by Nijō Tameyo. 2,143 poems. No prefaces. Another offering of poems in the plain style.

16   *Shoku goshūishū* (Later Collection of Gleanings Continued, 1326). Compiled on the order of Emperor Go-Daigo (1288–1339) by Nijō Tamefuji and, after Tamefuji's sudden death in 1324, Nijō Tamesada. 1353 poems. No prefaces. Another Nijō collection.

17   *Fūgashū* (Collection of Elegance, 1344–1347). Compiled under the aegis of Retired Emperor Hanazono, with much of the actual work done by Retired Emperor Kōgon and three fellows: Ōgimachi Kinkage (1297–1360) and Monk Kentetsu (precise dates unknown), who had both been wards of Kyōgoku Tamekane in earlier years, and Reizei Tamehide. 2,211 poems. Japanese and Chinese prefaces by Retired Emperor Hanazono. The second and last of the Kyōgoku-Reizei collections.

18   *Shin senzaishū* (New Collection of a Thousand Years, 1359). Compiled on the order of the Ashikaga shōgun Takauji (1305–1358) via Emperor Go-Kōgon (1338–1374) by Nijō Tamesada. 2,365 poems. No prefaces. The project was almost abandoned upon the death of Takauji, until Tonna convinced the new shōgun, Yoshiakira (1330–1367), to go on. Basically a Nijō collection favoring contemporary poets, albeit with some poems by emperors Fushimi, Hanazono, Kōgon, and a few Kyōgoku poets, including Tamekane; but no poems by Reizei Tamehide or any members of the Southern Court.

19   *Shin shūishū* (New Collection of Gleanings, 1364). Compiled on the order of the Ashikaga shōgun Yoshiakira via Emperor Go-Kōgon by Nijō Tameakira, and after Tameakira's death in 1364 by the monk Tonna. 1,920 poems. No prefaces. A Nijō collection.

20   *Shin goshūishū* (New Later Collection of Gleanings, 1383). Compiled on the order of the Ashikaga shōgun Yoshimitsu (1358–1408) via Emperor Go-Enyū (1358–1393) by Nijō Tametō (1341–1381), and after Tametō's death by Nijō Tameshige and a group of fellows. 1,554 poems. Japanese preface by Nijō Yoshimoto. Criticized for its inclusion of many poets from warrior families, almost all of them with direct ties to the Nijō house.

21   *Shin zokukokinshū* (New Collection of Ancient and Modern Times Continued, 1439). Compiled on the order of the Ashikaga shōgun Yoshinori (1394–1441) via Emperor Go-Hanazono (1419–1470) by Asukai Masayo, with the monk Gyōkō as librarian, and a number of fellows. Japanese and Chinese prefaces by Ichijō Kaneyoshi (1402–1481). Last of the imperial anthologies, although attempts were made later to produce a twenty-second. A partisan effort by the Nijō faction repre-

sented by the Asukai family and Gyōkō, with no representation whatsoever of Reizei Mochitame (1401–1454) or Shōtetsu.

22   *Shin'yōshū* (New Collection of Leaves, 1381). Early manuscripts compiled on the request of Emperor Go-Murakami (1328–1368) by Prince Munenaga and Kazan'in Nagachika; accepted as quasi-imperial anthology by Emperor Chōkei (1343–1394). 1,426 poems. Japanese preface by Prince Munenaga. No Chinese preface. Poems in the Nijō style by the royal family and courtiers of the Southern Court. Unusual in that it contains only poems by rough contemporaries and none by great poets of earlier eras.

ABBREVIATIONS AND BIBLIOGRAPHY

Place of publication is Tokyo unless otherwise stated.

Collections: Abbreviations

* Large collections.

+ Imperial anthologies. All numbers following these abbreviations in the text refer to those in [*Shimpen*] *Kokka taikan,* Taniyama Shigeru et al., eds., vol. 1. (Kadokawa Shoten, 1983).

BF   *Bofū guginshū* (Gyōkō), in *ST* 5.

DT   *Dainagon Tamesada shū* (Nijō Tamesada), in *ST* 5.

FG   *Fushimi'in goshū* (Emperor Fushimi), in *ST* 5.

+FGS   *Fūgashū* (1346).

FYS   *Fujigayatsu shū* (Reizei Tamesuke), in *ST* 5.

GDSS   *Gon-Daisōzu Shinkei shū* (Shinkei), in *ST* 6.

GGS   *Gyokuginshū* (Fujiwara no Ietaka), in *ST* 3.

GHN   *Gyōkō hōshi nikki* (Gyōkō), in *ST* 5.

*GR   [*Shinkō*] *Gunsho ruijū,* Hanawa Hokinoichi, comp., and Kawamata Keiichi, ed. 2d ed. 24 vols. Meichō Fukyū-Kai, 1977–1978.

+GSIS   *Goshūishū* (1086).

+GSS   *Gosenshū* (951).

+GYS   *Gyokuyōshū* (1312).

JS   *Jōben shū* (Jōben), in *ST* 5.

JW   *Jittei waka* (Shinkei), in *ST* 6.

KHS   *Kenkō hōshi shū* (Yoshida no Kenkō), in *ST* 5.

KIS   *Kōgon'in shū* (Retired-Emperor Kōgon), in *ST* 5.

+KKS *Kokinshū (905)*.

KUHS *Keiun hōin shū* (Keiun), in *ST* 5.

+KYS *Kin'yōshū* (1127).

MYS   *Man'yōshū* (mid-eighth century), in *SKKT* 2.

*NKBT *Nihon koten bungaku taikei*, Takagi Ichinosuke et al., eds. 102 vols. Iwanami Shoten, 1956–1968.

*NKT   *Nihon kagaku taikei*, Sasaki Nobutsuna et al., eds. 4th ed. 10 vols. 5 supplementary vols. Kazama Shobō, 1977–1981.

*NST   *Nihon shisō taikei*, Hayashiya Tatsusaburō et al., eds. 67 vols. Iwanami Shoten, 1970–1982.

REW   *Rin'ei wakashū*, in *GR* 7.

RS   *Rikashū* (Prince Munenaga), in *ST* 5.

RW   *Ryūfū wakashū*, in *GR* 7.

SAISSS *Saishōsō* (Sanjōnishi Sanetaka), in *ST* 7, part 2.

+SCSS *Shin chokusenshū* (1234).

SETSGS *Setsugyokushū* (Sanjōnishi Sanetaka), in *ST* 7.

SG   *Shūi gusō* (Fujiwara no Teika), *ST* 4.

SGS   *Sōga shū* (Asukai Masayori), in *ST* 5.

+SGSIS *Shin goshūishū* (1383).

+SGSS *Shin gosenshū* (1303).

+SHOKUGSIS *Shoku goshūishū* (1325).

+SHOKUGSS *Shoku gosenshū* (1251).

SHOKUGYW *Shoku genyō wakashū*, in *GR* 7.

+SHOKUKKS *Shoku kokinshū* (1265).

+SHOKUSIS *Shoku shūishū* (1278).

SHOKUSS *Shoku sōanshū* (Tonna), in *ST* 5.

+SHOKUSZS *Shoku senzaishū* (1320).

+SIS   *Shūishū* (c.a. 1006)

+SKKS   *Shin kokinshū* (1206).

*SKKT   *Shikashū hen*. Vol. 4 of [*Shimpen*] *Kokkan Taikan*, Taniyama Shigeru et al., eds. 5 vols. Kadokawa Shoten, 1986.

+SKS   *Shikashū* (1151–1153).

SM   *Shunmusō* (Shōhaku), in *ST* 7.

SŌGIS   *Sōgi shū* (Sōgi), in *ST* 6.

SOKS   *Sōkonshū* (Shōtetsu), in *ST* 5.

SS   *Sōanshū* (Tonna), in *ST* 5.

SSH   *Shinkei Sōzu hyakushu* (Shinkei), in *SKKT* 4.

+SSIS   *Shin shūishū* (1364).

+SSZS   *Shin senzaishū* (1356).

*ST   *Shikashū taisei*, Waka-shi Kenkyū-kai, ed. 8 vols. Meiji Shoin, 1973–1976.

SYS   *Shin'yōshū*. (1381)

+SZKKS   *Shin zokukokinshū* (1439)

+SZS   *Senzaishū* (1187).

TAE   *Tameshige Ason eisō* (Nijō Tameshige), in *ST* 5.

TS   *Tamemasa senshu* (Reizei Tamemasa), in *SKKT* 4.

TTS   *Tō no Tsuneyori shū* (Tō no Tsuneyori), in *ST* 6.

WRS   *Wakan rōei shū*, in *SKKT* 2.

*ZGR   *Zoku Gunsho ruijū*, Hanawa Hokinoichi and Hanawa Tadatomi, comps. 3d. rev. ed. 71 vols. Zoku Gunsho Ruijū Kansei-Kai, 1974–1975.

Other Poetry Collections and Editions

Eifuku mon'in hyakuban go-jika-awase, in *SKKT* 5.

[*Shakuchū*] *Fujiwara Teika zenkashū*, ed. Kubota Jun. 2 vols. Kawade Shobō Shinsha, 1985–1986.

Fūgashū, Iwasa Miyoko and Tsugita Kasumi, eds. Chūsei no bungaku series. 1st series, vol. 44. Miyai Shoten, 1974.

Goshūi wakashū, Fujimoto Kazue, ed. 4 vols. Kōdansha, 1983.

Kinkaishū, in *SKKT* 4.

Kokin waka rokujō, in *SKKT* 2.
Kokin wakashū, Ozawa Masao, ed. Nihon Koten bungaku zenshū series, vol. 7, Shōgakukan, 1971.
Man'yōshū, Kojima Noriyuki et al., eds. 4 vols. Nihon Koten bungaku zenshū series, vols. 2–5. Shōgakukan, 1971–1975.
Sankashū, in *SKKT* 3.
Shika wakashū zenshaku, Sugane Nobuyuki, ed. Kasama Shoin, 1983.
Shin chokusen wakashū kochūshaku to sono kenkyū, Ōtori Kazuma, ed. and comp. 2 vols. Shibunkaku, 1986.
Shinkei hyakushu waka, in Noguchi Eiichi and Yokoyama Shigeru, eds., *Shinkei shū*. Kisshōsha, 1946.
Shin kokin wakashū, Minemura Fumito, ed. Nihon koten bungaku zenshū series, vol. 26. Shōgakukan, 1974.
Tamemasa senshu, in *SKH/SKKT* 4.
Tameshige Ason eisō, in *ST* 5.
Tō no Tsuneyori shū, in *ST* 6.

Dictionaries and Reference Works

Nihon bungaku-shi, Hisamatsu Sen'ichi and Ichiko Teiji, eds. Rev. ed. 7 vols. Shibundō, 1977.
Nihon koten bungaku daijiten, Ichiko Teiji et al., comps. 6 vols. Iwanami Shoten, 1984.
Waka bungaku daijiten, Kubota Utsuho et al., comps. Meiji Shoin, 1962.
Waka bungaku jiten, Ariyoshi Tamotsu, comp. Ōfusha, 1982.
Waka kanshō jiten, Fujihira Haruo, Kubota Shōichirō, and Yamaji Heishirō, comps. Tōkyōdō, 1970.
Waka no kaishaku to kanshō jiten, Inoue Muneo et al., comps. Ōbunsha, 1979.

Waka Treatises, Critical Works, and Various Other Genres

Go-Toba-In kuden, Hisamatsu Sen'ichi, ed., in *NKBT* 65.
Gumon kenchū, in *NKT* 5.
Izayoi nikki, in Takei Kazuto and Yanase Kazuo, eds. *Izayoi nikki, Yoru no tsuru*. Izumi Shoin, 1986.
Kinrai fūtei, in *NKT* 5.
Michiyukiburi, in *GR* 15.
Nomori no kagami, in *NKT* 4. (Poems numbered in *SKKT* 5.)
Oi no kurigoto, Shimazu Tadao, ed., in *NST* 23.
Rakusho roken, in *NKT* 5. (Poems numbered in *SKKT* 5.)

Ryōshun isshiden (alternate title: *Ryōshun benyōshō*), in *NKT* 5. (Poems numbered in *SKKT* 5.)
Saki no sesshō-ke uta-awase, in *ZGR* 15, part 2.
Sasamegoto, Kidō Saizō, ed., in *NKBT* 66.
Seiashō, in *NKT* 5.
Shirakawa kikō, in Kaneko Kinjirō, ed., *Sōgi tabi no ki shichū*. Ōfūsha, 1976.
Shōtetsu monogatari, Hisamatsu Sen'ichi, ed., in *NKBT* 65.
Tōyashū kikigaki, in *NKT* 5. (Poems numbered in *SKKT* 5.)
Waka teikin, in *NKT* 4.
Yakumo kuden, in *NKT* 3.
Yoru no tsuru, in *NKT* 3.
Yoshimitsu-kō Itsukushima mōde no ki, in *GR* 15.

Studies and Translations

Araki Hisashi. 1977. *Imagawa Ryōshun no kenkyū*. Kasama Shoin.
Brower, Robert H. 1972. "Ex-Emperor Go-Toba's Secret Teachings: *Go-Toba no In Gokuden*." *Harvard Journal of Asiatic Studies* 32:5–70.
—— 1981. "The Reizei Family Documents." *Monumenta Nipponica* 36(4):445–461.
—— 1985. "Fujiwara Teika's *Maigetsushō*." *Monumenta Nipponica* 40(4):399–425.
—— 1987. "The Foremost Style of Poetic Composition: Fujiwara Tameie's *Eiga no Ittei*," *Monumenta Nipponica* 42(4):391–429.
Brower, Robert H. and Earl Miner. 1961. *Japanese Court Poetry*. Stanford: Stanford University Press.
—— 1967. *Fujiwara Teika's Superior Poems of Our Time: A Thirteenth-Century Poetic Treatise and Sequence*. Stanford: Stanford University Press.
Fujihira Haruo. 1983. *Shinkokin to sono zengo*. Kasama Shoin.
Hanser, Richard. 1966. "A Plea for Literary Mayhem." In Jerome W. Archer and Joseph Shwartz, eds., *Exposition*. New York: McGraw-Hill.
Hisamatsu Sen'ichi. 1978. *Chūsei wakashi ron*. Rev. ed. Hanawa Shobō.
Huey, Robert N. 1987. "The Kingyoku Poetry Contest." *Monumenta Nipponica* 42(3):299–330.
Huey, Robert N. and Susan Matisoff. 1985. "Lord Tamekane's Notes on Poetry: *Tamekane-kyō wakashō*," *Monumenta Nipponica* 40(2):127–146.
Inada Toshinori. 1978. *Shōtetsu no kenkyū: Chūsei kajin no kenkyū*. Kasama Shoin.

Inoue Muneo. 1984. *Chūsei kadanshi no kenkyū, Muromachi zenki*. Rev. ed. Kazama Shobō.

Ishida Yoshisada. 1943. *Tonna, Keiun*. Sanseidō.

Itō Sei. 1970. *Tanizaki Jun'ichirō no bungaku*. Chūō Kōronsha.

Iwasa Miyoko. 1976. *Eifuku Mon'in: Sono sei to uta*. Kasama Shoin.

—— 1979. *Ametsuchi no kokoro: Fushimi-In go-uta hyōshaku*. Kasama Shoin.

—— 1984. *Kyōgokuha kajin no kenkyū*. Kasama Shoin.

Keene, Donald. 1967. *Essays in Idleness: The Tsurezuregusa of Kenkō*. New York: Columbia University Press.

—— 1984. *Dawn to the West: Japanese Literature in the Modern Era, Fiction*. New York: Holt, Rinehart, and Winston.

Kubota Jun. 1976–1977. *Shinkokin wakashū zenhyōshaku*. 9 vols. Kōdansha.

—— 1984. *Fujiwara Teika: Ransei ni ka ari*. Ōchō no kajin series, vol. 9. Shūeisha.

Kubota Jun, ed. 1985–1986. *[Shakuchū] Fujiwara Teika zenkashū*. 2 vols. Kawade Shobō Shinsha.

Kubota Shōichirō et al. 1976. *Chūsei kinsei no kajin*. Waka bungaku kōza series, vol. 7. Ōfūsha.

Land, Myrick. 1983. *The Fine Art of Literary Mayhem*. San Francisco: Lexikos.

McCullough, Helen Craig, tr. 1985. *Kokin Wakashū: The First Imperial Anthology of Japanese Poetry*. Stanford: Stanford University Press.

Morris, Ivan. 1967. *The Pillow Book of Sei Shōnagon*. 2 vols. New York: Columbia University Press.

Reischauer, Edwin O. and Joseph K. Yamagiwa. 1951. *Translations from Early Japanese Literature*. Cambridge: Harvard University Press.

Seidensticker, Edward G. 1976. *The Tale of Genji*. 2 vols. New York: Knopf.

Shūka kanshō 1. 1976. Waka bungaku kōza series, vol. 10. Ōfūsha.

Takenishi Hiroko. 1972. *Shokushi Naishinnō, Eifuku Mon'in*. Nihon shijin sen series, vol. 14. Chikuma Shobō.

Toki Zenmaro. 1971. *Kyōgoku Tamekane*. Nihon shijin sen series, vol. 15. Chikuma Shobō.

Tsugita Kasumi. 1976. "Eifuku Mon'in," in *Chūsei, kinsei no kajin*. *Waka bungaka kōza* (Waka bungaku kai) 7:192–218.

Ueda Makoto. 1976. *Modern Japanese Writers and the Nature of Literature*. Stanford: Stanford University Press.

Yonehara Masayoshi. 1976. *Sengoku bushi to bungei no kenkyū*. Ōfūsha.

INDEX OF FIRST LINES
(JAPANESE)

Other Works in the
Columbia Asian Studies Series

Translations from the Asian Classics

Modern Asian Literature Series

Companions to Asian Studies

To Become a Sage: The Ten Diagrams on Sage Learning, by
    Yi T'oegye, ed. and trans. Michael C. Kalton   1988

The Message of the Mind in Neo-Confucian Thought, by
    Wm. Theodore de Bary   1989

Studies in Asian Culture

Introduction to Asian Civilizations
Wm. Theodore de Bary, Editor